Competition and Choice in the Publishing Industry

WALTER ALLAN

Publishing Director,
Institute of Economic Affairs

and

PETER CURWEN

Principal Lecturer,
Sheffield Business School,
and Shoemaker Scholar,
Penn State University

IEA

Published by
INSTITUTE OF ECONOMIC AFFAIRS
1991

First published in May 1991

by

THE INSTITUTE OF ECONOMIC AFFAIRS
2 Lord North Street, Westminster,
London SW1P 3LB

© THE INSTITUTE OF ECONOMIC AFFAIRS 1991

Hobart Paper 116

ISSN 0073-2818
ISBN 0-255 36245-5

*The Institute gratefully acknowledges financial support for its publications
programme and other work from a generous benefaction by the late
Alec and Beryl Warren.*

Printed in Great Britain by
GORON PRO-PRINT CO LTD
6 Marlborough Road, Churchill Industrial Estate, Lancing, W. Sussex

Text set in Berthold Baskerville

CONTENTS

FOREWORD

Every *Hobart Paper* published by the Institute of Economic Affairs has a common theme—how to make the best possible use of scarce resources. Although this theme has usually been developed while taking as given the existing framework of laws and institutions which govern the disposition of property, the process of exchange in the market-place, and the form and enforcement of contracts, these institutional features have sometimes been challenged. The purpose of this challenge has not been to dispute the aims of these laws—the choice of aims is not readily susceptible to economic analysis—but rather to argue that, given the aims, the framework of laws is, in the particular case analysed, ill-designed to achieve them.

This *Hobart Paper*, the 116th in the series, is in that latter group. It considers the Net Book Agreement, and argues that that Agreement does not serve the interests of the consumer.

Under the Agreement, publishers of books can set the price at which so-called Net Books—any books deemed by their publisher to be within the scope of the Agreement—may be sold to the public. Since the abolition of general resale price maintenance in Britain in 1964, the goods for which manufacturers can behave in that way have been few. This ending of a general restriction on competition has benefitted the consumer. Choice has been expanded, as retailers became free to choose what combination of service and price they would use to attract customers, and, as is pointed out in this *Hobart Paper*, the same has happened in every country where such restrictions on competition were abolished. It would be hard to maintain that the benefits of increased competition were a purely chance outcome, not to be expected in general. The conclusion to which the economic analysis of competition leads—that competition is beneficial to the consumer—is supported by evidence from different countries and different times.

Why not, then, have competition in books?

How is the Net Book Agreement defended? Several arguments have been advanced. It was maintained that without the Agreement, there would be a fall in the number of bookshops which held substantial stocks of books. This of course would restrict choice as consumers would thus tend to find out about books only through advertisements, as well as having to wait for books to be ordered and delivered. There would be a rise in book prices. And finally, there would be a fall in the number of books published, a fall which would be particularly marked among those books not aimed at a large market.

The authors of this *Paper* examine these defences both analytically and empirically, and conclude that, whatever merit they may have had when accepted by the Restrictive Practices Court in 1962, they can no longer be maintained. A fascinating, and particularly telling, part of this examination is contained in the discussion of 'The Book Trade Overseas'. This section has been written on the basis of the extensive experience in commercial publishing of one of the *Paper's* authors. It exposes as nonsense the belief that bookselling in the USA has, as a result of freedom to compete, become dominated by the marketing of 'best-sellers', with access to a wide range of books restricted and in many locations non-existent. The authors' arguments for the ending of the Net Book Agreement are well worth attention.

The Institute of Economic Affairs is a research and educational trust. It does not engage in advocacy; its trustees, directors, and advisers therefore dissociate themselves from the analyses and conclusions of the Institute's authors. It offers this *Paper* as an excellent example of the power of economic analysis in combination with the careful use of evidence to reveal how markets work, and how their institutions can be reformed to the benefit of the consumer.

May 1991   GEOFFREY E. WOOD
                                    City University Business School
                                                    IEA Trustee

THE AUTHORS

WALTER ALLAN was educated at Hawick High School and is an economics graduate of Heriot-Watt University. He is Publishing Director of the Institute of Economic Affairs. He was previously a teacher of Economics at Repton School, and has held senior publishing posts with Allen & Unwin and Macmillan Press. He is the author of *Concise A Level Economics* and *Concise O Level Business Studies*. For several years he was an examiner for the Oxford and Cambridge Board 'A'-Level Applied Economics Paper, and is currently a member of the Advisory Council for Housing Choice.

PETER CURWEN obtained his bachelor's degree in economics at the University of Liverpool in 1967, and after a period with Esso Petroleum he obtained his MBA at the Liverpool Business School in 1970. He has been Principal Lecturer in Economics at Sheffield Business School since 1986. He has been a visiting professor at universities in Germany, Spain and the USA, most recently at Penn State. He is well known for his work on the publishing industry, especially *The UK Publishing Industry* (Pergamon, 1980), and on public enterprise. He is also a prolific textbook author, most recently with *Understanding the UK Economy* (Macmillan, 1990).

INTRODUCTION

In February 1960, the Institute of Economic Affairs published the first of their series of *Hobart Papers*.[1] With hindsight this proved to be one of the most distinguished and influential *Hobart Papers* ever produced. In examining the arguments for and against resale price maintenance (RPM), Professor B. S. Yamey convinced the independent reader that the abolition of this practice would lead to an average reduction in retail prices of about 5 per cent.

Such was the impact of this *Paper* that by the end of 1963, the Government was seeking to abolish RPM. On 15 January 1964, Edward Heath (Secretary of State for Industry, Trade and Regional Development and President of the Board of Trade) informed the House of Commons of proposed legislation which would affect monopolies, mergers and resale price maintenance. On RPM, he stated:

> 'The Government believe that this practice is, in general, incompatible with their objective of encouraging effective competition and keeping down costs and prices. They have reached the conclusion that resale price maintenance should be perceived to be against the public interest unless in any particular case it is proved to the contrary to the satisfaction of a judicial tribunal.'[2]

Despite the stormy passage the Bill received in Parliament, The Resale Prices Act was passed into law in July 1964. By an ironic twist of fate, it was later claimed in some Tory circles that it was this enactment which led to the election defeat of the same year.

However, there is no doubt that since the abolition of RPM, consumers in the UK have enjoyed a wider range of goods and services at more competitive prices. The best example of this is in the Fast Moving Consumer Goods sector (FMCGs). Food retailers have enjoyed a phenomenal growth rate in the past 25 years, with big brand names such as Sainsbury, Tesco, Asda and Waitrose becoming household names.

[1] B. S. Yamey, *Resale Price Maintenance and Shoppers' Choice*.

[2] *Parliamentary Debates (Hansard)*, House of Commons, 15 January 1964, col. 225.

At the time it was feared that the small independent retailer would be forced out of business because he did not have the buying power of the large multiples. On the contrary, over the years the small independent retailer has been able in practice to survive either by diversification or by giving his customers a more flexible service.

One industry which was exempted from the requirements of the Act and which still adheres to Resale Price Maintenance is Publishing and Bookselling. Under the Net Book Agreement, the publishers—that is, the manufacturers—still set the price of their books and the booksellers (retailers) are not allowed to compete on price. As a result the industry has not changed a great deal since the early 1960s.

The expansion of libraries which were primarily publicly funded soaked up 2,500 copies of practically any book which was published. The 1970s and early 1980s witnessed a decline in real spending by libraries. In order to retain their profit margins, publishers drastically cut print-runs but prices of books increased and the number of titles published also increased to maintain turnover. The recession of the early 1980s did not affect the publishing industry in the same way as other industries. Mergers and takeovers became the order of the day as companies sought to achieve distributional and marketing economies of scale in the lead up to 1992.

With print-runs already cut to the absolute minimum, consumers are simply not prepared to pay the excessive prices which are now being asked for new books. As a result, in early 1991, a large number of redundancies within the book trade were announced; as long as restrictive practices continue, there seems little immediate prospect for the industry to expand.

Of course, no one can be sure of what would have happened in the absence of the Net Book Agreement, although the statistics in Table 1 hardly support the view that the NBA has kept prices down.

As can be seen, the increase in the general price of books has continued to outpace the Retail Prices Index throughout the 1980s.

For this and other reasons detailed in this *Paper*, there is, therefore, no sound economic argument for Resale Price Maintenance to remain in the publishing industry.

If this *Paper* is driven by historical events, or lacks extensive footnotes and references, we make no apologies. The industry

TABLE 1

BOOK PRICE INFLATION COMPARED
WITH THE RPI, 1981-88

| | (1981 = 100) | |
	Book Price Inflation Index	Index of Retail Prices
1981	100	100
1982	113	109
1983	119	114
1984	119	119
1985	134	126
1986	137	131
1987	153	136
1988	162	143
1989	N/A	N/A
1990	N/A	N/A

Source: Prima Europe Policy Research.

has been dominated for too long by 'The Hampstead Socialists' whose vested interests have been to preserve the *status quo*. As a result, there has been little in the way of scholarly material in the intervening period, and therefore few commentaries, critical or otherwise, about the publishing industry.

I. AN OVERVIEW OF THE NET BOOK AGREEMENT

Historical Retrospect

The earliest attempt to organise the book trade occurred in 1812 when London booksellers attempted to form their own association in order to forestall an increasing tendency to compete vigorously on price. Both this, and a second attempt in 1828, were failures, and although a further attempt was made in 1848, this coincided with the Free Trade Movement and led to an arbitration conference in 1852 at which Lord Campbell ruled that publishers could neither prescribe retail prices nor refuse to supply booksellers who undercut them. Little progress was made during the ensuing four decades, but Frederick Macmillan persevered in his opposition to underselling and in 1890 netted 16 books, the most significant of which was Alfred Marshall's *Principles of Economics*. In January 1895, the Associated Booksellers of Great Britain and Ireland was formed, followed exactly one year later by the formation of the Publishers' Association, and these two bodies agreed in 1897 that net books should not be sold at less than the published price. Agreement by the Society of Authors was not forthcoming, however, until 1899, and it was not until January 1900, therefore, that the first Net Book Agreement came into operation.

The Agreement was strengthened in 1906 when it was further agreed that a net book should not be sold as second-hand within six months of publication, and that new net books should not be reduced in price for a year. This was to prevent booksellers from using the pretext that a book was shopsoiled or had previously been sold in order to sell at less than the net price.

The current format of the Net Book Agreement (NBA), which is set out in the Appendix, was first introduced in 1957, shortly after the passing of the 1956 Restrictive Practices Act. This Act prohibited collective enforcement of restrictive practices, but exempted individual enforcement. The NBA, being an example of the former, was investigated by the Restrictive Practices Court, and a lengthy Judgement[1] was delivered on

---

[1] Hereinafter referred to as 'the 1962 Judgement' or simply 'the Judgement'.

30 October 1962 which, for the reasons set out below, allowed the Agreement to stand. Although the Resale Prices Act was passed in 1964 outlawing individual enforcement of resale price maintenance, exemptions under the 1956 Act were allowed to stand unless a significant change in trade practice could be proven to have taken place in the interim period. The NBA was accordingly allowed to retain its exemption by default, and its significance in law lies primarily in the fact that only one other exemption has subsequently been granted, that for branded drugs in 1970, and that agreement is now, for practical purposes, unenforceable.

'Books Are Different'

In the course of his Judgement, Mr Justice Buckley uttered the now famous words 'Books are different', sentiments with which the publishing industry concurred wholeheartedly. Unfortunately, the economics profession just as wholeheartedly rejected the Judgement as erroneous, and the controversy thus engendered has never fully died down. In the sections below we must accordingly consider, firstly, whether the Judgement was appropriate in the light of trade circumstances *at the time* and, more importantly, whether the NBA can still be justified in the light of *current* trade practice.

In the latter respect, it should be noted that the NBA has not come under attack purely from economists of a free market disposition. The Consumers' Association, for example, thought the existence of the NBA of such potential detriment to the public that it pursued its own investigation (Consumers' Association, 1978) which concluded that

'. . . on the evidence we have, the consumer, and the trade, would benefit from the freer competition which would follow from the ending of the Net Book Agreement'.[1]

Furthermore, in January 1988, the Monopolies and Mergers Commission, in its report on the proposed merger of Book Club Associates and Leisure Circle, commented in its conclusions:

'As a final observation, we hope that the Director General will keep developments in the book market under review. The book club market nowadays functions with great emphasis on simultaneous publication and introductory offers in formats identical, or

[1] *The Net Book Agreement: A Which? Campaign Report*, London: Consumers' Association, 1978, p. 22.

practically so, to the original publisher's editions. Such a special market in discounted hardbacks to some extent owes its existence to the Net Book Agreement, which prevents the discounting of publishers' ordinary editions. In the course of our enquiry we have noted that some of the conditions which prevailed when that Agreement was tested before the Restrictive Practices Court in 1962 no longer apply (paragraph 3.4 *et seq.*). The Director General might, in the exercise of his duties under the Restrictive Trade Practices legislation, consider whether there were grounds to review the Agreement after 25 years of operation.'[1]

It may also be noted that a recent ruling by the European Commission (12 December 1988) held that the NBA constituted an infringement of Article 85 of the Treaty of Rome to the extent that it covers the book trade between member-states. As a consequence, anyone taking a day-trip to France can stock up with discounted copies of English-language best-sellers from the hypermarket.

Finally, the past year has witnessed a concerted assault upon the NBA from within the book trade itself. Initially this took the form of the special Christmas promotion in 1989 of cut-price (albeit non-net) books by the Pentos group, owner of Dillons bookshops. Subsequently, on Saturday, 13 October 1990, Dillons took the unprecedented step of offering a 25 per cent reduction on the cover price of all the six titles which were short-listed for the Booker Prize, literary fiction's most prestigious award.

Commenting at the time, Mr Terry Maher, the Chairman of Pentos, said:

'Our action today is a result of mounting frustration and anger. There is now overwhelming public support for abolition of the NBA and there is an increasing desire for change within the trade. The entrenched interests of the book trade have totally failed to take any initiative to reform the NBA, despite the obvious fact that it is riddled with contradictions and anomalies.'[2]

The Agreement and the Industry

The NBA is binding upon those members of the Publishers' Association who publish net books, and concerns the conditions

---

[1] Monopolies and Mergers Commission, *Book Club Associates and Leisure Circle: A Report on the Merger Situation*, Cm. 277, London: HMSO, 1988, para. 6.42.

[2] 12 October 1990. Dillons announced that its bookstores would sell each of the six books shortlisted for the Booker Prize 1990 at a discount of over 25 per cent.

of sale relating to net books as defined in the Appendix. Such books cannot, other than in exceptional circumstances, be sold by booksellers at below the net prices fixed by the publishers for at least the first year after publication. The Agreement is intended primarily to defend the interests of the so-called stockholding booksellers who, in general, hold in stock more than 10,000 different titles. This permits the public to purchase direct from stock, and to browse through a collection of related items in pursuit of a publication which precisely fits their requirements.

The turnover of stock items tends to be high for general books in December, and for academic books in September/October. Nevertheless, a stockholding bookseller must expect to hold a large proportion of his stock in the form of slow-moving items. He must also (except in London) expect to subscribe, sight unseen, to many new books before they are published. In 1962, it was not customary for a publisher to offer a sale-or-return facility on such subscriptions, so that the bookseller effectively carried a significant part of the risk inherent in publishing books by unknown authors.

In 1960, some 24,000 books were published, some 16,000 for the first time. Since even a stockholding bookseller cannot be expected to hold more than a small proportion of these in stock, a good deal of his time is taken up in tracing and ordering books for customers. To be efficient in this respect, the bookseller needs to have a specialised knowledge. However, although the NBA does not prohibit a bookseller from charging for his services, customers tend to react adversely to such charges.

Booksellers buy from publishers at a discount off the net price. In 1962, the discount was $33\frac{1}{3}$ per cent for most general books including fiction; 25 per cent for most technical and educational books; and $16\frac{1}{3}$ per cent for more specialised books, including special orders. The rate of discount on export orders, which constituted approximately half of a typical publisher's sales, varied between 40 and 50 per cent. These rates of discount enabled few booksellers to make more than very modest profits, and there was an appreciable turnover of members of the bookselling trade.

The Judgement

Summary

The Restrictive Practices Court accepted more or less in its entirety the case made out in support of the Agreement. It accepted that the termination of the Agreement would lead to

○ fewer and less well-equipped stockholding bookshops;

○ more expensive books;

○ fewer published titles;

and that each of these consequences would arise in a sufficiently serious degree to make its avoidance a substantial advantage. The Court had certain reservations about possible trends in book prices were the Agreement to be terminated because it represented a state of affairs of which there was no experience or parallel at that time. Nevertheless, the Court held that no real evidence had been presented to support the view that on the balance of probabilities retail prices generally would fall.

The Court also rejected claims by the Registrar under the balancing provision (see Appendix, p. 73) that any benefits arising from the Agreement would be negated by other associated detriments. It argued, firstly, that the Agreement did not reduce the incentive to publishers and booksellers to keep down costs because the competitive nature of the publishing industry forced publishers to be cost-efficient in order to survive, and because the small profit margin enjoyed by stockholding bookshops left them little latitude for inefficiency.

Secondly, the Court argued that the Agreement did not deprive booksellers of opportunities to dispose of stock at their discretion, nor the public of opportunities to buy more cheaply because such a facility exists in the Standard Conditions of Sale (item (ii)) and in the existence of the National Book Sale. The Court also rejected the claim that prices were being maintained at artificially high levels, and that by protecting margins the Agreement compelled the public to pay more for books than would otherwise be the case. Finally, the Court did not believe that the Agreement prevented libraries and similar purchasers from negotiating advantageous terms with their suppliers.

II. ANALYSIS OF THE JUDGEMENT

Detailed Provisions

It is desirable to consider some of the points made in the Judgement in more detail if we are to assess whether the Judgement still holds good. Those with hardy dispositions can, of course, inspect the entire transcript of the case in Barker and Davies (1966). Before we begin, however, some general observations are in order. In the first place, it should be noted that the NBA is agreed by a group of signatory *publishers*. It is not an agreement between publishers and booksellers, nor amongst booksellers alone. Nevertheless, its avowed purpose is to protect the interests of stockholding booksellers.

Secondly, it must be remembered that a publisher has absolute freedom, both to designate a book as either net or non-net, and to transfer it from one category to the other at any time. He also has absolute freedom to fix the net price at any level, and to sell a book to anyone whom he chooses to supply at any price he so wishes. Thus the NBA is not at all representative of the type of restrictive practice commonly investigated by the Court. Furthermore, there are laid-down circumstances which permit a bookseller to sell a book at less than the net price. Aside from Standard Condition item (ii) (see Appendix, p. 73), the main provision is for an annual two-week National Book Sale during which any licensed bookseller may offer any book which he has not ordered during the previous 12 months at less than two-thirds of its net price or at its buying-in cost to the bookseller, whichever is less.

Thirdly, there exists the Library Agreement, set up in 1929, which authorises public libraries to obtain a library licence from the Publishers' Association. This licence entitles libraries to a 10 per cent discount on purchases from designated booksellers. The Library Agreement was set up in order to prevent those libraries with large budgets from demanding such high discounts from booksellers that the latter could make little or no profit from the business once their costs were taken into account. It was widely accepted in the trade that the termination of the NBA would result in the concession of higher discounts to most libraries.

As we have seen above, the Court accepted the view that the termination of the NBA would lead to higher rather than lower prices. This was chiefly because, firstly, if publishers could not rely upon stockholding bookshops to subscribe to, stock and display their books, they would have to be less adventurous about their publishing strategy. Certain books would not be published at all, and those that were published would have smaller print runs, thus forcing up unit costs and hence prices. In addition, booksellers' margins would be forced up through, for example, a refusal by booksellers to stock a given publisher's books except on more advantageous terms.

The Registrar's Arguments and the Court's Rejection of Them

The Registrar argued that the removal of a price restriction in the context of a competitive industry would lead to price reductions rather than the reverse. The Court held, however, that the Agreement served not as an instrument for fixing minimum prices, since the price of any individual book was determined independently, but as a device to preserve retail price stability. Furthermore, publishers would still have to recommend retail prices in order to establish the discounted price at which they would sell to booksellers, and there was a tradition whereby book buyers expected to buy books at the prices printed on their covers. Hence, price-cutting would be selective rather than widespread, and would frequently manifest itself as a form of loss-leadership whereby a general store might offer bargain-price books in order to attract custom to the store. This would, in the Court's view, serve merely to transfer demand from one outlet to another rather than to generate additional sales, with the result that booksellers would be afraid to hold large stocks of any book which might be used elsewhere as a loss-leader, subsequently forcing them to dispose of their holdings at a net loss. Furthermore, there was no reason to assume that any particular type of book would lend itself to loss-leadership.

The Court also held that, in the absence of the NBA, public libraries would either force higher discounts from booksellers, or would transfer their custom to specialised library suppliers, a factor which, when combined with selective price-cutting, would drive many stockholding booksellers out of business. Those who remained in business would hold smaller and less varied stocks, and would be forced to do more specialist orders which, because of the additional costs involved, would leave them with a negligible profit. In order to keep booksellers in existence, publishers would be forced to concede larger discounts which would push up prices unless they were able to reduce costs of production, as previously mentioned. Hence, although selected price-cutting would result from the termination of the Agreement, it would occur in the context of generally higher prices. Furthermore, although libraries would obtain larger discounts, these discounts would be deducted from higher prices, and libraries would gain little or no advantage in the long run. Eventually, a vicious circle would arise with higher prices leading to reduced demand; reduced demand to smaller print runs; smaller print runs to higher unit costs; and higher unit costs to higher prices.

The Court was not prepared to comment upon whether there was an excess supply of new books, a possibility denied by publishers. The Court felt that termination of the Agreement would lead to a reduction in the number of books published, the effects of which would be most severe in the higher reaches of literature. The Court felt strongly that this would deny to the public specific and substantial benefits.

The Court rejected the Registrar's contention that the Agreement served to preserve an antiquated system of book distribution. It held that there was nothing inherent in the Agreement to prevent innovation in methods, either of book distribution or of book production. Indeed, the competitive nature of the industry would ensure an adventurous approach in these respects.

Finally, the Court rejected the Registrar's contention that it was against the public interest for the bookseller to be forced to retain the whole of his discount irrespective of the services he offered or of his need for the discount, since he was effectively prevented from sharing this discount with the customer even where, for example, a book was simply bought straight off the shelf. The Court held that publishers fixed retail prices rather than discounts, and could if they so wished vary the discount to reflect the service provided by the retail outlet. However, it did not appear to be the case in practice that retail outlets other than stockholding booksellers were either willing or able to accept smaller discounts.

Commentary and Critique

The 1962 Judgement contained the argument that

'the degree to which booksellers share the publishers' risks by placing subscription orders, particularly for the classes of books which are of a more speculative kind, is considerable'.[1]

In general, it is a reasonable proposition that risk should be related to reward. In this case risk-sharing implied that the bookseller should not expect to be left with unsold stock because a rival had suddenly cut his prices on those titles, nor be forced to engage in a price war which would cause him to become unprofitable. The NBA effectively protected the bookseller against these possibilities.

But precisely what risks were being run in practice? In an early commentary on the Judgement, Professor B. S. Yamey[2] pointed out that, whereas the Court expected price-cutting in the absence of the NBA to be only *occasional* and *selective*, it expected the interests of consumers to be affected in a *far-reaching* way. He felt that this lack of symmetry disguised the fact that the additional uncertainty engendered by selective price-cutting would affect stockholding practice only to an insignificant degree, and could be compensated for by a slightly higher margin of discount on slow-moving stock. Since such stock would not itself be vulnerable to periodic price competition, it would remain economically viable to produce. The question of the relationship between discounts and stockturn would certainly appear to be a fundamental issue. In 1962 the Registrar's economist, Professor C. F. Carter, argued that

'the distributor should enjoy a larger margin on stock which is likely to be slow to move (and may not be sold at all) and a smaller one on stock which moves fast'.[3]

At the time trade practice was (as indeed it still is) based upon a diametrically-opposed principle, namely that the risk was greatest in the case of a potential best-seller where the print run was typically longer and the royalty typically higher as compared to an academic text. For the textbook, the market was reasonably well-assured even in the absence of heavy bookshop exposure, whereas in the case of the 'best-seller', exposure and availability were all-important so that the bookseller had to be rewarded for ordering a large stock in case the book turned out to be a flop and the stock

1 *Reports of Restrictive Practice Cases*, Vol. II, 1961-63, pp. 246-327, Incorporated Council of Law Reporting for England and Wales, 1963, p. 260.

2 'The Net Book Agreement', *Modern Law Review*, November 1963, pp. 691-9; also *Resale Price Maintenance and Shoppers' Choice*, Hobart Paper No. 1, Second Postscript to the Third Edition, London: Institute of Economic Affairs, January 1964, especially p. 55.

3 *Reports of Restrictive Practice Cases, op. cit.*

was therefore left unsold on the shelves. The publishers' economist argued that it was inappropriate to examine best-seller profitability after the event, since in the case of an individual title the risks were being run *before* sales took place. In his view the bookseller assessed the degree of risk at the *margin* when deciding how much of any title to stock, and related this to the discount offered so that an increased rate of discount on a particular book would make the ordering of additional copies desirable (i.e. potentially profitable), which it would have been too risky to order at a lower discount.

In accepting these arguments the Court ruled that

'rates have been evolved by ordinary economic processes in the course of many years of business, and broadly represent the margins which publishers find necessary to induce booksellers to stock and endeavour to sell their products'.[1]

Rather interestingly this implies, as noted elsewhere, that the rate of discount offered by a publisher on a given title is such as to render that title economically viable in its own right, whereas publishers continue to argue that best-sellers subsidise the higher reaches of literature.

'Sale or Return' . . .

Changes in trade practice since 1962 have given cause to re-examine the merits of the above arguments. In particular, it is now customary to offer books to stockholding booksellers on a 'sale or return' basis. Such a facility reduces greatly the risk inherent in subscribing to a given type of book, and therefore enhances the original argument of the Registrar's economist that the discount should be related to the rate of turnover. On many occasions a retail outlet may simply have some racks which are filled with the latest batch of titles, with the old titles removed for remaindering or destruction. This involves the retailer in no direct risks whatsoever, and it is difficult to see why the retailer should expect a high rate of discount under such circumstances. A high discount should constitute either a reward for exceptional risk to the retailer or for an exceptional level of service offered by the retailer. In the case of direct supply, both risk and service are negligible. This suggests that in the absence of the NBA, the stockholding bookseller who provides a full service should simply be given a higher rather than a lower rate of discount, thus permitting him to compete on price.

[1] *Op. cit.*, p. 297.

III. THE NET BOOK AGREEMENT AND RESALE PRICE MAINTENANCE

Introduction to Resale Price Maintenance

The purpose of the NBA is to ensure that such books as are designated to be 'net' by publishers are not sold at lower prices. Given that an individual publisher cannot be expected to monitor the prices at which his entire list is sold at every retail outlet, he obviously needs to be party to a formal agreement which covers both his own and other publishers' net books.

It may be argued that the practical effect of having such an agreement in force is to induce publishers to designate the great bulk of their titles as net books, except insofar as a particular group of titles, such as school textbooks, is traditionally not so designated. Hence, whilst the NBA is not an agreement between publishers to fix minimum prices in collusion, it does at times appear to lead to much the same outcome, as noted below (p. 42).

Nevertheless, the NBA is sensibly treated, for analytical purposes, as a specific form of resale price maintenance (RPM). The purpose of RPM is to allow a producer to fix retail prices which he deems to be in *his* own best interests, and thereby to deny to retailers the right to fix prices which they deem to be in *their* own best interests. In general, this can be expected to lead to a higher level of prices than would otherwise exist (because it prohibits the possibility of price competition between retailers), and to leave retailers with a higher retail margin. This, in turn, given that price competition is ruled out, is likely to be partly translated into improved levels of service, more advertising and promotion, and improvements to premises. The substitution of non-price for price competition is against the interests of consumers who have no say in the matter, and is widely regarded as such a severe detriment as to lead to the outlawing of RPM in the UK and most similar countries.

The whole purpose of the free market is to allow firms to compete. Where a firm is more efficient than another it can earn the same profit margin at a lower level of prices. Prices therefore tend to fall in efficient firms, leaving the inefficient the option either of becoming more efficient and surviving or of going out of business.

Non-Price Competition

This does not imply that only the cheapest suppliers will survive, since that will only be true where consumer preferences are uniquely a function of retail prices. In practice, non-price competition may be of value to consumers, some of whom will accordingly be prepared to pay higher prices for a better quality of service. The key point is that the free market will force firms to provide their preferred quality of service as cheaply as possible, and that the range of different types of services on offer will be determined by the preferences of consumers rather than of suppliers.

In the specific context of publishing, non-price competition is likely to take a number of forms such as

o stocking titles for which there is very limited demand;

o the provision of bibliographic advice without charge even though it is labour-intensive;

o the provision of a free-of-charge special ordering service for titles not held in stock;

o the provision of books to libraries at a price which does not reflect the full costs of the service.

Innovation is also likely to be stifled by RPM since any savings which arise as a direct result cannot be passed on in the form of lower prices to consumers. Hence a bookseller with innovative ideas has little opportunity to gain market share at the expense of his stodgier rivals, and retailing techniques lag behind those in sectors not subject to RPM. This argument presumes that lower prices will cause customers to switch from high-priced to low-priced outlets, which must remain an unproven hypothesis in the UK publishing industry so long as RPM remains in force. It is, however, an appealing hypothesis as a matter of simple logic, and there is much evidence to support it in sectors not subject to RPM.

Are Price Wars Detrimental to Consumers?

It may be counter-argued that over-reliance on price competition is a de-stabilising influence. RPM eliminates the possibility of price wars which would ultimately have drawbacks for consumers since prices would, on average, end up higher. This arises because retailers would compensate for increased

[23]

uncertainty by reducing orders for stocks and by demanding higher margins in order, firstly, to increase their chances of surviving a price war and, secondly, to make price reductions appear more impressive. These factors would raise costs and hence prices. However, whilst the abolition of RPM did lead to short-term instability in other retail sectors, there is no real evidence to suggest that it has of itself resulted in constant, let alone de-stabilising, price wars.[1]

A further potential consumer detriment could arise as a consequence of the abolition of RPM insofar as it would result in the acquisition of monopoly power by the winners in a price war. In the context of the book industry, however, the recent trend to increased concentration in both publishing and book-selling renders it most unlikely that any one imprint or bookshop chain would see anything to be gained in engaging in a price war intended to drive others out of business.

Other factors, such as the possibility of obtaining books via mail order or book clubs, would also militate against the abuse of market power at retail outlets, as would the ability of new entrants to offer effective competition, albeit not in the short term for reasons set out below.

Is the NBA a Price-Fixing Agreement?

The Restrictive Practices Court was influenced by the apparent fact that publishers set prices competitively, and hence concluded that the NBA did not operate as a price-fixing agreement. According to Mr Justice Buckley:

'. . . it must be borne in mind that the agreement is not a price-fixing agreement. Its object is not the maintenance of any particular prices or price level throughout the trade or any section of it. Net prices are fixed by publishers in conditions of free competition. The main object of the agreement is, in our view, to preserve retail price stability; it is not an instrument for fixing prices.'[2]

Regrettably, the Court did not appear to have learned very much about the workings of the free market. It is evident, to begin with, that every book is by its very nature unique, and hence no two books can be regarded as perfect substitutes. On the other hand, it is evident that every title is substitutable by

---

[1] See T. Calvani and J. Largenfeld, 'An overview of the current debate on resale price maintenance', *Contemporary Policy Issues*, Spring 1985.

[2] *Reports of Restrictive Practice Cases*, *op. cit.*, p. 312.

other titles to a greater or lesser degree. A title will not be unique insofar as

○ it is out of copyright and there are different publishers' versions of that title;

○ the customer is looking for a title by a specific author, but regards other books by that author as equally acceptable;

○ the subject matter is descriptive or technical, and is covered in much the same way in other texts (possibly written by the same author);

○ the customer is looking without prejudice for, say, a children's book with pretty illustrations.

It appears to be the case, therefore, that a title rarely faces so little competition that its publisher has absolute discretion over the price which he sets. The name of a best-selling author does confer an element of monopoly power, but it is inadvisable to price such an author noticeably above the going rate for 'No. 1 best-sellers' given that such books are typically bought in outlets such as airports where customers are often looking for a 'good read' rather than a specific title, and soon notice if certain titles are relatively expensive. Equally, however, it is risky for a publisher to try to undercut the going rate since additional sales cannot be relied upon to compensate for the reduction in price. Bearing in mind that the retailer cannot discount the publisher's price under the NBA, the most sensible strategy for a publisher is to charge the 'going rate' for, say, a mass-market paperback, and periodically to try to push it upwards in the hope that other publishers will follow suit.

The one certain thing in publishing is that if a particular title proves to be a best-seller, other publishers will be unable to produce a new product at a cheaper price to compete with it. Even if a publisher thought that he could bring out a cheaper alternative, written on a similar topic by an author of similar reputation, the time lapse before such a book could reach the market would normally negate the point of such an exercise.

In general, given the existence of the NBA, we would expect publishers to price similar products as though they were operating a cartel. The fact that they can fix the price of a specific title at any level they wish is very far from what is meant by 'conditions of free competition'. In conditions of free competition there would be constant downward pressure upon prices in

[25]

order to clear the market, so that over time prices, on average, would rise more slowly than elsewhere in the economy where free competition did not exist. As is demonstrated in Section VII on book prices, there is no evidence to support such an assertion.

Contestability

In recent years the concept of 'contestability' has been introduced to counteract the above line of argument. Dr Frank Fishwick, of the Cranfield Management School, for example, introduces the concept of contestability into his analysis.[1] A contestable market is one where an opportunistic seller can enter the market without incurring costs which are irrevocable should the entrant subsequently choose to exit the market. According to Dr Fishwick,

> 'Book publishing and retailing are relatively easy to enter and leave— the book market is contestable. If book publishers or booksellers made great profits by exploitation or (a more realistic allegation) operated an inefficient trade reflected in unnecessarily high costs, what is to stop other companies from coming in and doing things differently?'[2]

Given that even the proverbial 'man in the street' can sub-contract the various processes involved in publishing a book, such as editorial services and printing, the apparent answer to this question is 'nothing'. It is evident, however, that distribution is an awkward issue since neither a stockholding bookshop nor a supermarket will stock a title produced in this way, and mail order is not a viable alternative—at least in terms of offering real competition to established publishers. Dr Fishwick suggests that new entrants could take the form of press groups, able to use magazine distribution systems and sell via Confectioners, Tobacconists and Newsagents (CTNs) and supermarkets. As it happens, many such groups are already involved in the publishing business so the competition they represent is actual rather than threatened.

In any event, a contestable market requires ready-made products to contest with, and books have to be written before they can be produced, let alone distributed. One of the essential points about those markets claimed to be contestable is that the

---

[1] F. Fishwick, *The Economic Implications of the Net Book Agreement*, London: The Publishers' Association, 1989.

[2] *Ibid.*, p. 43.

potential entrant can lay his hands on everything he needs at a moment's notice. In the case of publishing this is simply not the case since, whereas there are indubitably a vast number of unpublished manuscripts in existence, the sheer volume of what is already published does not suggest that those which are discarded can, without at best significant revision, offer any real competition to the existing products.

In bookselling it is easier to be contestable since one has merely to lease a retail premises and order stocks from publishers. Nevertheless, suitable premises are rarely so easy to acquire at short notice in the real world, and they may well need substantial refitting costs to attract customers which would constitute irrevocable costs to the retailer should he choose to leave the industry. An existing retailer of other products could, in principle, switch shelf space over to books from other products, but the fact that he would undercut existing book-sellers by so doing is not the same thing as assuming that he would make more profits by selling books compared with his previous product range.

If the market is indeed highly competitive, then we would expect profitability to be relatively modest in publishing and bookselling. If published accounts are to be believed this is indeed the case in the UK, but there is no reason to assume that abolition of the NBA would make matters worse. Recent experience in the USA, discussed subsequently (below, pp. 63-66), indicates strongly that the roots of the problem lie elsewhere, particularly in the churning out of titles with no realistic possibility of breaking even combined with excessive advances for best-selling titles which increasingly fail to recover those advances. Furthermore, the restructuring of book retailing in the UK has been held back by the existence of the NBA. Attributing low profitability to an excess of competition is, accordingly, wholly unsatisfactory.

The NBA and Cultural Diversity

There can be no doubting that books have a special cultural, social and educational rôle to play. There are those who believe that these considerations are so strong that if the NBA helps to ensure cultural diversity, it should be kept in force even in the face of potent economic grounds for its abolition.

It has long been received wisdom in publishing circles that popular titles of little literary or cultural merit cross-subsidise more 'worthy' titles which would be hopelessly uneconomic to publish were such cross-subsidisation not to occur. This view was not only voiced during the case before the Restrictive Practices Court but, in particular, during the unsuccessful defence of RPM in Australia; in the resolution passed by the European Parliament favouring fixed book prices in 1981;[1] in the discussion underpinning the introduction of RPM in France; and whenever it is proposed to reintroduce RPM in areas where it has previously been abolished.

In view of the above, it is important to question, firstly, whether cross-subsidisation is indeed a direct consequence of RPM and, secondly, whether this should be viewed as a positive or negative attribute of RPM. This latter point is the more straightforward of the two. As indicated, the defence of RPM in Australia was unsuccessful, partly because the cross-subsidisation argument was used as evidence *against* RPM. This was because, in a free market, price is meant to reflect the value placed upon a commodity by the consumer, and cross-subsidisation clearly distorts consumer choice by inducing consumers to buy fewer 'unworthy' titles and more 'worthy' titles than they would in its absence.

Free-market principles are much more in vogue currently than they were in the 1960s, so it is fair to say that the advocates of RPM would be ill-advised to push the cultural argument were the NBA to be reappraised. In any event, there are awkward redistributional issues to be addressed since 'unworthy' titles are predominantly read by a different, poorer, segment of society than that which reads 'worthy' titles.

The issue as to whether cross-subsidisation is a consequence of RPM is difficult to prove either way, at least in the absence of considerable additional research. The key point to bear in mind is that cross-subsidisation is necessary only if publishers and booksellers set out deliberately to make a loss on certain titles. This could occur because the NBA guarantees a high rate of return on stocking best-sellers, and that guarantee provides the means to cross-subsidise other titles which are held in stock even though they are expected to lose money.

Now it is possible to argue that many booksellers are happy to make a modest living from their businesses, and choose to stock

---

[1] 'Resolution on the fixing of book prices' (13 February 1981), *Official Journal of the European Communities*, No. C50/103, 9 March 1981.

slow-moving titles which they believe consumers 'ought' to be reading. It does not seem probable, however, that they want to go bankrupt, in which case they must have a reasonable expectation that the great majority of titles stocked will make at least *some* profit.

That being so, if any title suddenly became much less profitable, that would be the title which would not be stocked. Hence, if discounting were to be permitted, and heavy discounts were offered on best-sellers at other outlets, the sensible strategy for the affected bookseller would be to reduce orders for those titles rather than for the slow-movers whose profitability is not under threat. Indeed, logic suggests that it would pay many stockholding bookshops to leave the heavily discounted sector of the market to those outlets which wanted to stock them exclusively, and to concentrate on acquiring a reputation as a specialist supplier of, for example, academic/professional texts.

IV. A REVIEW OF THE UK PUBLISHING INDUSTRY

The Economics of Publishing

In theory, the publishing industry should approach perfect competition. There are many buyers and sellers; in the UK alone some 60,000 titles are published each year. In practice, it is an oligopolistic market, protected by high entry costs, restrictive practices and market imperfections.

Whitaker & Son, the publishers of *Books in Print* and the weekly trade journal, *The Bookseller*, estimate that there are almost 15,000 publishers in the UK but only 400 are members of The Publishers' Association.

In the early 1980s, it was estimated that 70 per cent of the books published in the UK were by the leading 10 publishing houses. The merger boom of the mid-1980s led to the creation of the 'Big Four' who probably now account for 50 per cent of the total domestic book trade. These four large publishing groups are:

o *HarperCollins*: part of the Murdoch News International empire and was created when Rupert Murdoch took control of Harper & Row Inc., a major US academic and business publisher, and William Collins, an old-established UK publishing house which had been in some financial difficulty at the start of the decade.

o *Reed International*: receive most of their turnover from Octopus Books and Heinemann. Octopus Books was founded by Paul Hamlyn, one of the great post-war independent publishing entrepreneurs, and acquired the Heinemann list, a well-respected academic and schools publisher, in the mid-1980s. The group also controls Butterworth, the prestigious central London-based law publisher.

o *The Pearson Group*: probably best known as publisher of *The Financial Times* but the acquisition of the Longman Group in the 1970s and Penguin Books in the 1980s gave it a strong market presence in both the educational and trade market. Addison-Wesley, the US-based academic publisher, is also a Pearson imprint.

o *Random House*: a private US publisher, is the largest trade publisher in the UK and operates under the name of Random Century following the takeover of Century Hutchison. It is particularly strong in fiction and its imprints include Chatto & Windus, Jonathan Cape and Bodley Head.

*　　　　*　　　　*

The purpose of this section is to provide an insight into the Anglo-American publishing industry and to explore ways in which the price of books, which bears little relation to cost, can be reduced to a level where copies will be bought more by individuals than by libraries and academic institutions.

(i) Academic Publishing

There seems to be very little to choose between the mainstream academic publishing houses on prices, print-runs, quality of the products, advances and numbers of copies sold.

Why does an academic choose Publisher A instead of Publisher B? In the main, the choice depends upon the relationship between an author and the publisher's editor. The reputation of the publishing house in any particular academic discipline is governed by how the editor is viewed by his or her authors. It is often said that it takes six months to find out that an editor cannot do his job but three years to find out that he can. Unfortunately, good editors tend to be poached by rival publishers and there is normally a merry-go-round every three years. Many authors have found to their cost that the initiating editor is not the person who is finally responsible for publishing the book.

The First-Time Author

A young PhD student seeking to publish his first thesis is normally advised to approach one of the 'Ivy League' University Presses. In the USA, he has a choice between Harvard, Yale, Princeton, Stanford, Columbia and a host of other university presses. However, in the UK Oxford and Cambridge University Presses are still seen by academic peers as the imprints with which to have one's first work published.

The University Presses enjoy the luxury of charitable status and do not face the demands of shareholders looking for a return on their investment. They also operate a policy of cross-

TABLE 2

INCOME/EXPENDITURE ACCOUNT: FIRST-TIME AUTHOR

Expenditure (gross)		Income (net)	
Manufacturing Cost (800 copies @ £5)	£4,000	UK Sales (100 copies)	£1,950
Royalty	£1,455	Europe (150)	£2,700
Promotion	£1,000	Japan (150)	£2,700
Profit Margin 55%	£8,095	USA (300)	£6,300
		Commonwealth (50)	£900
	£14,550		£14,550

subsidisation, whereby a title with little commercial appeal will be given the green light if it is seen as a scholarly piece of work.

A scholarly work published, say, by Cambridge University Press, will have a print-run of perhaps 750-800 copies for an 80,000-word monograph. The average price for such a work is in the region of £30. If the book exceeds 100,000 words (about 300 pages or so) or has large chunks of mathematics or tabular matter, the price will currently be nearer to £35.

It is customary to mark up manufacturing cost by a multiple of six for academic titles. In other words, a book published at a price of £30 would have a unit cost of about £5. Thus, a publisher printing 1,000 copies of the book in the initial print-run would be faced with a printer's bill of £5,000. The income/expenditure account for a typical monograph with world rights might be as in the example shown in Table 2.

The manufacturing cost is based on a print-run of 800 copies, because 50 or so copies will be absorbed in reviews, author's copies, copyright libraries, representatives' samples, and so on.

Royalty payments are calculated on the basis of 10 per cent of *net* receipts. It is unlikely that an advance will be paid on such a publication since the decision to publish will only have been taken after the manuscript has been completed.

In Table 2 the number of copies sold in each region is shown in brackets and the discounts given are as follows: UK 35 per cent, Europe and Japan 40 per cent, USA 30 per cent and Commonwealth 40 per cent.

TABLE 3

LIFE-CYCLE SALES PATTERN: FIRST-TIME AUTHOR

		£
Year 1	70%	10,185
Year 2	20%	2,910
Year 3	10%	1,455
		14,550

The life-cycle of such a publication will usually be three years and the sales pattern over this period is approximately 70:20:10. From a cash-flow point of view, the amount publishers will receive is shown in Table 3.

In an average year, a University Press might publish 400 new titles. This is pure 'vanity' publication. At £30 per copy, very few individuals will buy the book. The international academic library market (primarily publicly funded) will absorb the 750 copies which are sold.

The Mature Academic

It is very rare for academics who have written several books to have stayed with the same publisher. The publishing houses who provide the academic with his first published work rarely offer the service for the author looking to sell 3,000 copies of his work. The experienced author is entitled to know what the expected print-run and price of his book will be. An editor who withholds this information is either not aware of the true market potential or is being 'economical with the truth'.

This is an area of the market where authors are often badly let down. Of the big four, HarperCollins, Reed and the Pearson Group have acquired prestigious academic imprints in order to reach their dominant market position. A title selling 3,000 copies is unlikely to generate an income greater than £50,000 and so they are not prepared to invest much effort (in capital or man-hours) towards generating such a relatively small income. The independent academic publisher is able to provide the author with the level of personal service he requires, but does not have the financial strength to ensure that the book is reviewed in the

TABLE 4

INCOME/EXPENDITURE ACCOUNT OF BOOK
BY ESTABLISHED AUTHOR

Expenditure (gross)		Income (net)	
Manufacturing Cost (3,250 copies)	£9,750	UK (750 copies)	£9,750
Advance	£2,000	Europe (750)	£9,000
Royalty	£1,055	Japan (400)	£4,800
Promotion	£3,000	Commonwealth (100)	£1,000
Profit Margin 48%	£14,745	USA (1,000)	£6,000
	£30,550		£30,550

national press or that the author appears on a television 'chat' show.

Very few publishers of UK origin can sell more than 1,000 copies of a book in the USA. If they do, it is because they have sold the US rights. When that happens, the author can expect to receive a much smaller royalty on his US sales. At the current sterling/dollar exchange rate, US publishers are buying the rights for 70 per cent discount off the UK list price. Under net receipt royalty arrangements, this equates to a list price royalty of 3 per cent (i.e. 10 per cent of 30 per cent).

The example given in Table 4 is based on an independent UK publisher who sells the US rights of an academic book to an American university press and the book is written by a well-known academic on a subject which would be of some interest to the general reader. The published price is £20.

On the income side, units sold have increased to 3,000 but higher discounts have to be offered to encourage more general bookstores to stock the book. The profitability of the US deal looks slim but there is a significant cash-flow advantage. The £6,000 generated by selling the US rights will be paid within 90-120 days which is the normal credit term in the printing industry. *Thus almost 65 per cent of manufacturing cost is paid for in advance.*

The manufacturing cost is also a much lower percentage of the published price, since unit cost goes down significantly as the

TABLE 5

SALES PATTERN OF A POPULAR TEXTBOOK

		No. of copies sold
Year 1		10,000
2		7,000
3		5,000
4		3,000
5	New Edition	7,500

print-run expands. Promotion cost is now a larger proportion of income (say, up to 10 per cent), with a launch party in, for example, a Pall Mall club accounting for the bulk of this amount.

The Textbook

This is the easiest book to criticise but the most difficult one to write. Apart from Samuelson[1] and Lipsey,[2] very few textbooks have travelled internationally. Those that do usually originate in the United States where the most successful texts sell well in excess of 100,000 copies. In the UK, 10,000 copies would be regarded as very successful.

If we consider the intermediate text, the life-cycle should be four years but the publisher will have spent much more on marketing, may have given out 1,000 copies as 'inspection copies', and will have offered the author a sliding-scale royalty, since strong selling textbooks are the most profitable part of a publisher's list.

The sales pattern of a popular textbook might read as in the example in Table 5.

There are three reasons why sales decline with each new edition. Firstly, second-hand bookshops are full of textbooks sold by students who no longer have any need for them. Secondly, some textbooks are liable to date quickly and may move from recommended to supplementary reading lists. Finally, any textbook which is selling 10,000 copies per annum is bound to attract a competitor to bring out a rival publication.

[1] Paul A. Samuelson, *Economics: An Introductory Analysis*, New York: McGraw-Hill, First Edition 1948, 13th Edition 1989.

[2] R. G. Lipsey, *An Introduction to Positive Economics*, London: Weidenfeld & Nicolson, First Edition 1966, 7th Edition 1989.

[35]

TABLE 6

TEXTBOOK INCOME/EXPENDITURE ACCOUNT:
FIRST EDITION

	Year 1		
Expenditure (gross)		*Income (net)*	
Manufacturing Cost (20,000 copies)	£45,000	UK (10,000 copies)	£97,175
Advance	£5,000		
Royalty	£4,717		
Promotion	£20,000		
Profit Margin 23%	£22,458		
	£97,175		£97,175

	Year 2		
Expenditure (gross)		*Income (net)*	
Royalty (15% of net receipts)	£10,203	UK (7,000 copies)	£68,022
Promotion	£2,000		
Profit Margin 82%	£55,819		
	£68,022		£68,022

Taking the example of the textbook selling 10,000 copies in the first year, we will trace the income/expenditure account over the life of the first edition (Table 6). The list price is £14.95 and the royalty is 10 per cent of net receipts on 10,000 copies sold and 15 per cent of net receipts thereafter.

The textbook, therefore, represents a sizeable investment to a publishing house, but if the right 'product' is correctly marketed it is possible to generate an income of £250,000 over the life-cycle of the book. It is also possible that sales could be generated in the Commonwealth, but we have confined our example to the UK in order to simplify the accounting procedure.

A UK publishing house would be seeking a small return on its investment during the first year of publication. The launch of a similar product in the USA would undoubtedly run at a loss during its first year.

TABLE 6 (Continued)
TEXTBOOK INCOME/EXPENDITURE ACCOUNT:
FIRST EDITION

Year 3			
Expenditure (gross)		*Income (net)*	
Reprint (10,000 copies @ £2 per copy)	£20,000	UK (5,000 copies)	£48,587
Promotion	£2,000		
Royalty	£7,288		
Profit Margin 40%	£19,299		
	£48,587		£48,587

Year 4			
Expenditure (gross)		*Income (net)*	
Royalty	£4,372	UK (3,000 copies)	£29,152
Promotion	£2,000		
Profit Margin 78%	£22,780		
	£29,152		£29,152
Total Expenditure	£122,580		
Profit Margin 50%	£119,356		
	£242,936	Total Income	£242,936

(ii) Trade Publishing

To a certain extent, academic and educational publishing can work to a set formula. However, trade publishing is the area where the greatest profits and losses are made.

The book trade has enjoyed a boom period during the 1980s as living standards and leisure time have increased. As public sector spending on books has declined in real terms, around 75 per cent of publishers' turnover has ended up in the retail sector.

A large proportion of best sellers are now imported from the United States and most professional writers have agents. It is

TABLE 7

INCOME/EXPENDITURE ACCOUNT OF A 'BEST SELLER'

Expenditure (gross)		Income (net)	
Advance to Author	£100,000	UK Sales (50,000 at 40% discount)	£448,500
Promotion	£25,000	Serialisation	£20,000
Production (50,000 @ £2)	£100,000	Sales of Paperback Rights	£20,000
Profit Margin 55%	£273,500	Foreign Language Rights	£10,000
	£498,500		£498,500

customary for a popular trade title to be auctioned, which normally takes place in a central London hotel. An author, with the help of his agent, will invite a select number of trade publishers to bid for the UK rights of the title; each publisher will have worked out in advance the maximum it is prepared to pay.

A number of titles in the 1980s has exceeded a six-figure advance which bears absolutely no relation to the number of copies eventually sold. How can a trade publisher make money by paying a £100,000 advance whilst selling only 50,000 copies at £14.95? Table 7 illustrates the point that it can be done.

If we assume that the author is on 10 per cent of net receipt royalties, the unearned income on the advance is £55,150, with the author receiving 22 per cent of the net receipts. However, the sales of serialisation, paperback and foreign language rights just about cover this amount and still leave the publisher with a satisfactory rate of return. Once again, a discount of 40 per cent is assumed.

Production Cycle

In theory, a book should not take longer than 30 weeks to produce. If all goes according to plan the production schedule should take the route set out in Table 8.

In practice, three of these stages get clogged up. In the first place, the assistant editor will very rarely give the manuscript to a copy editor the day it comes in from the author.

TABLE 8

TYPICAL PRODUCTION SCHEDULE

		No. of weeks
Stage 1	Manuscript delivered	
Stage 2	Send to reviewers	4
Stage 3	Implement reviewer's comments	2
Stage 4	Copy edit	4
Stage 5	Typeset manuscript	4
Stage 6	Author checks proofs and index	2
Stage 7	Correction of proofs, etc.	2
Stage 8	Print and bind	6
Stage 9	In warehouse	6
		30

The typesetter is traditionally a one-man business on an industrial estate who is working at 120 per cent capacity in order to finance his expensive machines. Consequently, he does not begin to typeset the day the manuscript arrives at his factory.

At the same time, the printer is faced with publishers competing for his time. Since print runs are lower on academic titles, manufacturing unit cost is a larger proportion of total cost and a publisher may prefer to wait until a printer has spare capacity when he will be quoted a lower price for the job.

It is still not known why it is necessary to keep books in a warehouse for up to six weeks before publication. The traditional argument is that it takes time to send out review and sample copies, although distribution within the trade is still regarded as a disgrace by many booksellers.

Backlist and Front List Publishing

An unhealthy trend has emerged in recent years whereby publishers have become dependent primarily on front list publishing. This has led to an increase in the number of titles being published, bringing a glut of new titles on to the market. An excess supply under normal trading conditions leads to a reduction in price. This does not apply to publishing since as demand falls the print run is cut, and to retain profit margins the

TABLE 9

PRICING OF ACADEMIC BOOKS

Basil Blackwell
    Economics for Professional Examinations   £40
    International Trade   £40
    Modern Political Thought   £40

Macmillan Press
    Economic Policies in the Pacific   £40
    Transport in a Free Market Economy   £40
    Studies in Banking & International Finance   £40

Edward Elgar
    Power and Economic Institutions   £38·50
    Beyond Keynesianism   £35
    The Capitalist Economies   £35

Routledge
    Charging for Government   £35
    Economics and Hermeneutics   £35
    Japan and the Global Economy   £35

Oxford University Press
    The British Economy Since 1945   £35
    The British Population   £40
    The European Dynasty States   £35

Cambridge University Press
    European Integration Trade & Industry   £30
    Macro Economic Policy in Britain 1974-1987   £35
    Environmental Management in the Soviet Union   £30

---

price is increased. Sadly, we have now reached the £50 monograph in the United Kingdom. This vicious circle must come to a standstill soon since several publishers are now bringing out titles with a 400-copy print run. There are titles being published today which would have been rejected on sight 10 years ago, but inferior imprints desperate for new products have been eager to snap up what is not taken up by the more prestigious publishers.

Ideally, a publisher would like revenue derived 30 per cent from new titles and 70 per cent from backlist, and this has significant cash-flow implications. However, for many academic publishers the ratio is reversed, with one of the major players

TABLE 10
PRICING OF HARDBACK FICTION

Bloomsbury
    The Adultery Department   £13·99
    Rose Reason   £13·99
    Pious Secrets   £13·99

Jonathan Cape
    The Smile of the Lamb   £13·99
    Day of Atonement   £13·99
    Playing the Game   £13·99

Chatto
    Asya   £13·99
    Ramage   £13·99
    Indoor Boy   £13·99

Hamish Hamilton
    The Playroom   £13·99
    The Second Prison   £13·99
    Hornhill   £13·99

HarperCollins
    The Kitchen God's Wife   £13·99
    Acts of Worship   £13·99
    The Crown of Columbus   £13·99

Viking
    Two Lives   £13·99
    Regeneration   £13·99
    Elvis   £13·99

accounting for 90 per cent of turnover with titles produced in one year.

Under the Net Book Agreement there has been no price competition on the part of the publisher. Although no formal cartel exists within the academic presses, there is clear evidence to suggest that Basil Blackwell and Macmillan Press are seen as the price leaders, with other publishers willing to follow suit or price just below the price leaders.

Table 9 lists the titles which are to be published by six academic economics imprints in 1991 and which were advertised in the Spring issue of *The Bookseller* as their lead titles.

Among the hardback fiction houses, competing for the best

[41]

sellers, there is, once again, remarkable consistency in their pricing policies. Table 10 shows the result of taking three titles from each of six well-known brand names in this field.

Thus, in the absence of price competition, publishers operate what amounts to a cartel since books are geared to the going rate for a mass-market paperback or academic text. In competitive markets, costs must be reduced to maintain profit margins. The publishing industry has the luxury of raising prices in tandem to maintain this ratio.

V. ECONOMIC ISSUES

Elasticity

Given a normal downward-sloping demand curve, the removal of a minimum price restriction should cause price to fall and quantity demanded to rise. The 1962 Judgement held that the number of *suppliers* would fall and that prices would *rise*. It is evident, therefore, that the Court was making certain assumptions about the way the retail book market worked which are worth spelling out with care.

In the first place, any reduction in prices by one retail outlet would drive another out of business only if customers were both willing and able to shop around.[1] Given the fact that competing retail outlets are in close proximity in only a small number of towns, and that the saving to be made with respect to a single discounted book is insufficient to warrant much search effort, there is no reason to expect high elasticities to be a general characteristic of the market. The obvious circumstance in which the prediction of the Judgement might prove to be correct would be if consumers were made aware of the availability of discounted books, in advance of their purchases, by means of advertising (which would need to be other than in the bookshop itself to be effective). This proposition is supported by such limited evidence as exists in the USA and Australia (Fishwick, 1985). Even in cities with competing discounting bookshops in close proximity, most consumers apparently do not bother to shop around, possibly because certain full-price bookshops have more status value.

Furthermore, whilst this kind of advertising is designed to attract consumers to specific outlets, and away from others, it generally serves to stimulate demand for books in general. Hence full-price bookshops may obtain new customers to offset those who rush off in search of discounts, especially if the discounting bookshops are not easily accessible.

In the second place, the Court accepted that there was a low price elasticity of demand for books in general, or in other words

[1] This is known in technical economic language as a high cross-price elasticity of demand between outlets.

[43]

that total purchases of books were insensitive to the general level of book prices (i.e. that books are price inelastic). Whilst little is known for certain about this matter, no one has yet come up with any convincing evidence that the price elasticity of demand is less than unity. In other words, a one per cent reduction in price can be expected to lead to at least a one per cent increase in quantity demanded, and total bookshop receipts are accordingly more likely to rise than to fall as a consequence of price reductions. Receipts are not the same thing as profits, but the economics of the publishing industry are such as to lead one to expect profitability to rise faster than revenue.[1]

Finally, it is worth observing that, even if one were to accept the Court's pessimistic view about elasticities, price-cutting by one outlet would drive another outlet out of business only if the latter was unable to meet price competition head on. This would presumably be true only if the latter was less efficient than the former, and hence operating on a dangerously low profit margin. There is evidence to suggest that many UK bookshops do operate on undesirably low margins, but even if one were to accept the desirability of keeping inefficient outlets artificially in operation, one can as readily expect their position to improve as to deteriorate if the elasticity conditions are favourable.

The Court was concerned that the abolition of the NBA would put bookshops in a situation of great uncertainty due to the threat of price-cutting, which in turn would discourage the holding of stock. Given favourable elasticity conditions, the degree of uncertainty is much reduced, and if combined with sale-or-return clauses would suggest that the Court greatly overestimated the difficulties faced by booksellers compared with other retailers.

The Netting of Books

Great emphasis is placed upon the fact that the decision whether to make a book net or non-net is entirely voluntary. What is not altogether clear from much of the discussion is precisely who stands to benefit most from this decision. It is argued that the consequence of the NBA is to stabilise the book market and hence to maintain choice and sales, both of which are in the interests of consumers. However, it makes no sense at all to assume that the publisher's decision is driven by anything other than his own self-interest. Clearly, he must believe that the net

[1] See P. J. Curwen, *The UK Publishing Industry*, Oxford: Pergamon, 1981.

price is the most profitable price for himself. If he believed that the object of the exercise was to improve consumer welfare then he could simply reduce the price and create more sales.

Nevertheless, the publisher's profitability is partly dependent upon the relationship which holds with booksellers. Hence, if booksellers believe that the NBA is in their interests it must generally pay publishers to play along. This does not mean that all booksellers will support the NBA. For reasons set out elsewhere (p. 26), it is clear that the main beneficiaries of the NBA are the less efficient booksellers. The fact that many publishers are well aware of this would account for the phenomenon which Fishwick found to be 'puzzling' (Fishwick, 1989, p. 45), namely that a number of publishers of net books were 'strongly opposed to the NBA'. The fact that they continued to publish books net rather than non-net is readily explained by an understandable reluctance to be the first to break ranks, and by a fear that orders for non-net books would suffer as a consequence. Fishwick also makes much of the proposition that

'Where RPM is chosen voluntarily and independently by producers, this will benefit consumers provided that it leads to greater sales without any price increase'.[1]

Unfortunately, as demonstrated in Section VII below, so far as the UK is concerned that simply is not what happens in practice, so it follows that it cannot be consumers who are the winners.

Title Output

There has been an explosion of title output in the UK, as shown in Tables 11 and 12.

1988 was a record year for title output. 1989 was a record year for title output. 1990, for which data are as yet unavailable, is expected to break the previous record comfortably, probably by well over 10 per cent. Title output first reached 20,000 in 1957. It took 11 years to reach 30,000 and 11 more years (1979) to reach 40,000. Ten years later it had comfortably exceeded not 50,000 but 60,000.

It is interesting to note that in the USA, where the home market is five times larger, the number of new titles and new editions peaked in 1983, at a total of 53,400, and subsequently fell away rapidly with the result that title output is now much

[1] Fishwick (1989), p. 44.

TABLE 11

NEW TITLES PUBLISHED IN UK:
COMPARISON OF TOTALS, CLASSIFIED BY SUBJECT,
JANUARY – DECEMBER 1988 AND 1989

	1988	1989	+/-	% change
Art	1,703	1,757	+54	+3
Biography	2,131	2,150	+19	+1
Chemistry and Physics	839	1,068	+229	+27
Children's Books	5,063	6,217	+1,554	+23
Commerce	2,033	1,818	−215	−11
Education	1,429	1,499	+70	+4·9
Engineering	1,604	1,416	−188	−1
Fiction	6,496	7,221	+725	+11
History	2,153	2,205	+52	+2
Industry	456	600	+144	+31
Law and Public Administration	1,932	2,438	+506	+26
Literature	1,574	1,816	+242	+15
Medical Science	3,423	3,238	−185	−5
Natural Sciences	1,199	1,361	+162	+13
Political Science	4,307	4,444	+137	+3
Religion	2,047	2,186	+139	+7
School Textbooks	2,007	1,751	−256	−13
Sociology	1,284	1,468	+184	+14
Travel and Guide Books	1,333	1,396	+63	+4·7
Total new books	43,188	46,042	+2,854	+6·6
Total new editions	13,326	15,153	+1,827	+13·8
Overall total	56,514	61,195	+4,681	+8·3

Source: The Bookseller, 3 August 1990.

TABLE 12

TOTAL BOOK OUTPUT BY CLASS:
NUMBERS OF TITLES, 1989

Classification	January – December 1989			
	Total	Reprints and New Editions	Trans- lations	Limited Editions
Aeronautics	218	36	2	
Agriculture and Forestry	537	106	8	
Architecture	439	89	13	
Art	1,757	276	69	6
Astronomy	146	28	2	
Bibliography and Library Economy	621	110	1	
Biography	2,150	602	81	7
Chemistry and Physics	1,068	154	30	
Children's Books	6,217	1,537	192	3
Commerce	1,818	484	10	2
Customs, Costumes, Folklore	217	49	7	2
Domestic Science	860	244	11	
Education	1,499	279	3	
Engineering	1,416	327	15	
Entertainment	614	140	20	
Fiction	7,221	3,560	321	8
General	838	152	9	
Geography and Archaeology	718	238	14	
Geology and Meteorology	313	56	4	
History	2,205	487	63	1
Humour	262	31	1	
Industry	600	129	6	
Language	749	194	7	2
Law and Public Administration	2,438	603	19	
Literature	1,816	273	69	1

[Table 12 contd. on p. 48]

TABLE 12 (Continued)
TOTAL BOOK OUTPUT BY CLASS:
NUMBERS OF TITLES, 1989

Classification	January – December 1989			
	Total	Reprints and New Editions	Trans- lations	Limited Editions
Mathematics	1,554	324	35	
Medical Science	3,238	718	31	1
Military Science	457	126	3	1
Music	469	130	17	
Natural Sciences	1,361	233	11	1
Occultism	481	114	15	1
Philosophy	729	127	69	
Photography	287	30	4	2
Plays	388	109	43	
Poetry	898	104	83	13
Political Science and Economics	4,444	852	52	
Psychology	1,014	199	20	
Religion and Theology	2,186	329	157	1
School Textbooks	1,751	254	21	2
Science, General	153	22	1	
Sociology	1,468	214	30	
Sports and Outdoor Games	913	242	5	3
Stockbreeding	321	75	6	1
Trade	697	165	1	
Travel and Guidebooks	1,396	535	17	1
Wireless and T.V.	253	67		
Totals	**61,195**	**15,153**	**1,598**	**59**

Source: The Bookseller, 3 August 1990.

TABLE 13
NEW TITLES (INCLUDING NEW EDITIONS AND REPRINTS)
PUBLISHED IN UK AND USA, 1960 TO 1990

	UK	USA
1960	16,472*	16,554
1965	19,506*	28,595
1970	22,755*	36,071
1975	35,608	39,372
1980	48,158	42,377
1985	52,994	50,070
1990	63,980	53,446

Sources: The Bookseller; Publishers Weekly.   * New titles only.

lower in the USA than in the UK (see Table 13). In part this may reflect the much greater dependency upon exports in the UK, although this has been true during the entire period. It is also undoubtedly the case that there must be some finite limit to the demand for greater variety, and that this is reached with a population size much smaller than that of the USA. Furthermore, unless the typical US bookshop holds a much larger stock than that of its UK equivalent, there is going to be enormous difficulty in acquiring bookshelf space for an ever-expanding number of titles.

However, if these latter arguments are valid, it is difficult to understand why the output of titles in the UK continues to grow so rapidly. The total UK population has been almost static for some time, with the result that there is now more than one new title each year for every 1,000 of the population.

'A Substantial Detriment'?

The fear expressed in the Judgement was that a 'substantial' detriment would arise were fewer books to be published. There are currently some 500,000 books in print, one for every 100 of the population. It is reasonable to suppose that the NBA has contributed to this proliferation of titles, which has not been a characteristic of countries where RPM on books is absent. Presumably, therefore, its abolition in the UK would cause title output to fall.

Publishers appear to have no qualms about publishing books

even where their prospects are severely constrained by the fact that they cover the same material for the same market as books already in existence. New technical books appear which are clearly inferior to existing texts, and plots in fiction books are rehashed *ad infinitum*. Superficially, such a publishing strategy would appear to be doomed to failure. However, there is some evidence, for example, the continuing profitability of firms such as Mills and Boon, that controlled duplication of proven formats may be the secret of success in particular markets. It is well known that the majority of loans from public libraries fall into categories such as romantic fiction, which suggests that some consumers would suffer some detriment were fewer titles in these categories to be published. On the other hand, there is no reason to suppose that this reduction will happen if demand is buoyant. Nevertheless, in other areas of publishing the consumer surely gains so little from duplication that the rejection of near-substitutes would offer up a larger share of the market for such books as are published, thereby enabling print runs to be longer and unit production costs and prices to be lower. Thus, overall, consumers would benefit in these areas, even though choice might be restricted, since lower prices would be viewed by the majority as preferable to a larger number of near-substitute books.

If fewer books were to be published, the reduction would not be in the categories where demand is buoyant. The Judgement identified a potential reduction in the higher reaches of literature without carefully defining this term. It seems more probable that the brunt of any reduction would be felt in the ranks of the cookery and gardening books, and US evidence suggests that literary works can sell well. In any event, there now exist alternative means of reaching a potential audience for academic/literary works with limited appeal other than via the traditional book.

VI. RETAILING ISSUES

Shopping Around

It is interesting to note how easy it is to turn the logic of a free market on its head when defending the NBA. It is held, for example, that a drawback to selective price-cutting is that it encourages potential purchasers to 'shop around'. Hence many purchases get to be postponed or even abandoned as customers move from outlet to outlet seeking bargains which in many cases do not exist. Evidently rational economic behaviour is perfectly acceptable for all products other than books. It is rather doubtful whether customers would spend a lot of time and effort trying to secure a discount amounting to a few pounds at best on a book, so such behaviour is only likely to occur where competing retail outlets are in close proximity. In any event, customers will then enter more than one outlet and, given the evidence on impulse buying, this should result in a greater probability of an unplanned purchase at one or other of the outlets rather than the reverse.

It is also suggested that the offering of discounts for multiple purchases would be disadvantageous for booksellers, even though it is not merely in common usage for other products but also for books in certain other countries such as Australia and Belgium. The reasoning behind this is that if orders are pooled, and a single individual is then sent to make the purchase, the number of potential customers will fall and turnover will be reduced. It is very difficult to understand who would behave in this way on such a scale as to more than wipe out the benefits of generating multiple orders. The pooling of textbook orders by students is put forward as one possibility, but the authors' experience suggests that this is generally beyond their organisational skills at the beginning of the academic year. Furthermore, their limited budgets do not suggest they spend any more money than is strictly necessary on recommended, let alone on unplanned, purchases.

It is argued that if prices were not fixed by the publisher, the retailer would be forced to make constant adjustments to the prices of his stock in line with changes by other competing

[51]

retailers. As there are so many titles compared to the product range carried by most other retailers, this would be especially burdensome and costly for booksellers. This argument contrasts somewhat with the point made in the Judgement, and reiterated constantly thereafter, that price-cutting would be selective. Hence only a modest number of titles would need to be monitored, and the utilisation of computerised data should facilitate this task and rectify any errors if stock already on the display shelves is incorrectly priced.

Implicit Discounting—Book Clubs and Own Brands

Explicit discounting of books is not permitted under the terms of the NBA. However, discounting has become an increasingly familiar phenomenon as a result of the growth of various forms of implicit discounting.

Since 1962 the practice of selling books via outlets other than stockholding bookshops has become increasingly prevalent. In particular, this has occurred via the expansion of book clubs in the UK. In their evidence to the Restrictive Practices Court, The Publishers' Association expressed some trepidation about the potential of book clubs to take business away from stockholding bookshops. At the time, book clubs accounted for roughly 1 per cent of publishers' domestic UK turnover.

Over the ensuing decades the book club bandwagon did indeed gain momentum, and publishers came increasingly to pander to the book club market, despite their initial reservations, even bringing out simultaneous hardback and book club editions at substantially different prices. In 1988 the Monopolies and Mergers Commission (MMC) attempted to estimate the size of the book club/mail order market. It could not come up with a precise figure, but it calculated for 1986 that

'book clubs and mail order may account for between 12 per cent and 19 per cent of the total value of book sales to individuals, and around 20 per cent of the total value of hardback sales to individuals'.[1]

The MMC attributed this growth in the book club market primarily to the existence of the NBA, which effectively prevented the development of bookshops selling recent titles at discounted prices.

---

[1] Cm. 277, *op. cit.*, p. 13.

Economic Effects of Book Clubs

Book clubs customarily buy in bulk at discounts well in excess of those available to bookshops, and then pass on part of these discounts to club members. But the discounts are in practice somewhat illusory because the cost of postage and packing, borne by the member, is necessarily high due to the weight of the product. The obvious benefits of book clubs lie, therefore, not so much in the ongoing discounts which are offered, since these are generally modest and are anyway tied to a very limited choice of titles, but rather in the introductory offers which are hugely discounted and in the provision of books for people who live in parts of the UK where there are no local bookselling outlets.

Book clubs clearly do mitigate the effects of the NBA in a modest way, and they have familiarised the reading public with the idea that books can be acquired at less than full retail price, but they are by no means a valid substitute for retail outlets selling discounted books. The choice is too limited (and the highly concentrated nature of club ownership also results in overlaps between the choices offered by apparently independent clubs) and is geared to the deals made between clubs and publishers. Discounts have to be traded off against the obligations to buy contained in the club rules (which are less onerous in the USA where similar books are discounted in retail outlets).

There can be no doubt that the termination of the NBA would be highly damaging to the book clubs because book buyers in larger towns would be able to buy more cheaply in discounting bookshops than from book clubs (after adjusting for costs of shipment). Nevertheless, prices are unlikely to be adversely affected. Book club orders from publishers serve to reduce unit costs and hence to bring down prices. A transfer of demand to discounting bookshops should serve to maintain and possibly to increase production runs.

'Own-Brand' Books

A second area in which book buyers have become indirectly familiar with discounting is through the publication of 'own-brand' books. These are produced for a variety of retail stores, such as Marks & Spencer and the large supermarket chains, but the main outlet is W. H. Smith, which sells large quantities of a limited range of books in its own shops (as well as being the owner of Sherratt and Hughes, a chain of stockholding bookshops).

Own-brand books are typically either children's books or non-fiction books aimed at the leisure market in areas such as cooking and gardening. The standard practice for most own-brand retailers is to have a special edition prepared exclusively for their use. These are, however, rarely original works. Most commonly they take the form of a repackaging of an existing book on sale elsewhere as a net book. Hence costs are relatively modest and they can be sold at a price well below that of the publisher's own version.

A more explicit example of discounting took place at Christmas 1989 when Dillons sold a range of books at well below their previous retail prices. As these were not net books, this piece of enterprise did not break the terms of the NBA. Nevertheless, what all of the above practices have in common is that essentially the same product is being sold at more than one price simultaneously. As the section below demonstrates, this has failed to bring about the dire outcome predicted in 1962, namely the partial destruction of retail bookselling.

Modern Bookselling in Practice

The implications of sale or return in transferring risk back from booksellers to publishers is that it must be in the interests of publishers to promote an expansion of bookselling outlets and of stocks held. The evidence from the USA set out elsewhere indicates that this can be expected to take place in the absence of RPM. The evidence from the UK, discussed below, indicates strongly that removal of the NBA would not damage the interests of the modern stockholding bookshop, which exists in a form rather different from that cited in the 1962 Judgement.

The passing of the Resale Prices Act 1964, subsequent to the 1962 Judgement, triggered far-reaching changes in retailing practices. The consequences for retail competition of removing RPM were at best cloudy at the time, given that the only experience of retailing in a free-market environment was to be found overseas, and this offered only a limited guide as to what might happen in the UK.[1]

In the event, experience subsequent to the 1964 Act has demonstrated that consumer demand can be readily stimulated

[1] B. S. Yamey, *Resale Price Maintenance and Shoppers' Choice*, Hobart Paper No. 1, London: Institute of Economic Affairs, First Edition 1960, Third Edition 1964.

through the provision of attractively laid out shops. Whilst this is not to deny the desirability of good service, most customers prefer to be able to look around for themselves in comfort before consulting shop assistants. The typical early-1960s bookshop did not provide an atmosphere conducive to browsing, and hence customers tended to walk out if they could not find what they had come in for. The Court acknowledged the rôle played by impulse buying in 1962, and modern bookshops are generally arranged so as to induce passers-by to enter the bookshop in the first place and to pick up titles other than those they may have expressly come to buy. Non-specific entry into modern bookshops represents a good third of all customers at the present time, and many of these (Dillons claims a figure of 40 per cent) make a purchase.

As usual, there is the virtuous circle element to consider. If bookshops are made more attractive at great cost (six-figure investments are no longer rare), more people will enter and more books will be sold, hence justifying the initial investment. Nevertheless, it is not permitted under the NBA to tempt potential customers to enter by virtue of advertised price reductions, and it follows that this must inhibit the volume of business. Modern, attractive bookshops stimulate the total market for books, as is demonstrated by experience in both the UK and the USA. They do not destroy the trade of other outlets. Such an outcome is only to be expected where the market has reached saturation, and it has yet to be argued that book-buying in the UK has reached that point. Indeed, it is well known that book-buying habits are better developed in almost every other Western nation.

The NBA has not prevented the introduction of improvements in bookselling altogether, but its removal must surely lead to an expansion of the customer base, many of whom will be buying books at full retail prices. Many of the most modern bookshops are parts of chains which have expanded enormously during the past decade, as shown in Tables 14 and 15.

Evidence before the Court in 1962 indicated that the 750 or so stockholding bookshops which existed at that time carried stocks ranging from 9,000 to 60,000 titles. In relation to the number of books in print at the time, the figure of 20,000 titles which appeared to be viewed as a respectable stock level was much higher than it would be currently with 500,000 titles in print. Nevertheless, the typically low level of stockholding under-

TABLE 14

BOOKSHOP MULTIPLES[1]: NUMBER OF BRANCHES, 1984-89

Group Name	1984	1985	1986	1987	1988	1989
Blackwells	39	44	48	55	51	56
Hammicks	11	15	15	20	26	30
Hatchards/Claude Gill	5	9	21	26	29	27
Pentos (Dillons and Athena Bookshops)	23	27	34	45	56	59
Sherratt & Hughes	31	34	38	44	48	54*⎫
Waterstones	5	7	13	22	30	34*⎭
Total	114	136	169	212	240	260

[1] Booksellers with five or more outlets and excluding W. H. Smith stores trading under that name.

* 88 after merging in 1988/89.

TABLE 15

BOOKSHOP TURNOVER OF MULTIPLES,
1983/4, 1987/8 AND 1988/9

	(£ million)		
	1983/84	1987/88	1988/89*
Hammicks	£4	£14	£15
Waterstones	£3	£29	⎫
Sherratt and Hughes	£4	£26	⎬ £75
Hatchards	£14	£24	£28
Pentos (Dillons and Athena Bookshops)	£8	£46	£60
Blackwells	£32	£42	£43·4
Total	£65	£181	£221·4

* Latest estimates per *The Bookseller*.

Source: *The Bookseller*.

standably conjured up a picture of a trade which would be vulnerable to damage were there to be the introduction of a de-stabilising influence such as the removal of the NBA.

The current situation is clearly very different. Only a relatively modest share of the overall bookselling market is accounted for by bookshops with a turnover of less than £250,000 per annum. As shown in Tables 14 and 15, turnover in the typical bookshop owned by the multiples has increased much more rapidly than the growth rate in the number of stores. This growth has, naturally, been supported by correspondingly larger levels of stock. The average Dillons stock is currently 100,000 titles, rising to almost 250,000 at their largest London store. Even given the significant increase in the number of titles in print since 1962, it is evident that the chain bookshops provide a much wider range of choice than existed at that time. Furthermore, there is less necessity to place orders for items not in stock, which is arguably just as well given the continuing evidence of excessive delivery times from publishers' warehouses.

Recent estimates by the Corporate Intelligence Group indicate that the volume of book sales is rising at approximately 8 per cent per annum, even in the absence of price competition. Unfortunately, as shown in the next section on book prices, this has been accompanied by sharp rises in the retail prices of books. Given the much-changed nature of the bookselling trade, there seems to be much less reason today than in 1962 to protect retail bookselling from the forces of the free market. Such protection is not available for other retailers and the interests of consumers do not appear to have been prejudiced as a consequence.

Consequences for Bookselling

It is probable that the abolition of the NBA will result in some restructuring of bookselling in the UK. This will, however, take the form of the inefficient going out of business and the efficient (whether new independents or additional branches of an existing chain) taking their place. There was a presumption in the 1962 Judgement that traditional stockholding bookshops (which as we have seen were not expected to hold a wide range of stock by current standards) would be the ones to suffer, and that these would not be replaced by an equal number of new entrants.

Experience in the USA has demonstrated, however, that

consumer preferences will ultimately determine the structure of the retail market and that traditional stockholding bookshops may ultimately be the growth sector rather than the reverse. In any event, the chain bookshop in the UK is generally more like a true stockholding bookshop than those cited in the Judgement. The fact that certain bookshops will go out of business should not, therefore, be a matter of great concern, since these are almost certainly going to be inefficient shops kept in business only by virtue of the NBA, whereas those which replace them will be viable in a free market.

VII. BOOK PRICES

Overview

As we have seen, there is considerable disagreement over the question as to whether book prices will rise or fall as a consequence of the abolition of the NBA. It is evident that, as happened subsequent to abolition in Sweden, Australia and France, its abolition in the UK will cause its supporters to rush out with evidence that prices have risen. However, this area is fraught with difficulties, and it is appropriate, therefore, to examine such statistics as exist currently in order to determine both how prices have moved during the past decade and also how much reliance can reasonably be placed upon the data.

Economic theory predicts that a major purpose—and a major consequence—of RPM is to keep prices higher than they would have been in the absence of RPM. Given that RPM either does or does not exist at any point in time, it is impossible to be certain about what would have happened had the opposite situation prevailed. In this case we can seek to measure how prices moved with RPM in operation, and we can compare this with the Retail Prices Index (RPI) which provides a rough-and-ready measure of the rate of inflation across the economy as a whole.

It must be admitted at the outset that the available statistics on book prices are to a greater or lesser extent flawed. In the first place, we really need to know not merely how book prices are changing but also the effects upon the volume of sales. This is because a book is not a homogeneous product, and measurement of an average price will almost certainly disguise switching between categories of book and from higher-priced to lower-priced books within a given category. Unfortunately, whilst the Publishers' Association produces statistics under the aegis of their Statistics Collection Scheme (PASCS) which take account of volume as well as price, these are based upon the revenue received by the publisher which is net of booksellers' discounts. Since the latter are themselves variable, it is impossible to extrapolate with any precision the actual shop prices paid by consumers. Other indices do not take volume changes into account at all.

Secondly, none of the price indices take into account any changes over time in the quality of books. In general, where quality is rising, prices are likely to rise more or less in line, but this omission is compounded by the fact that quality is not consistent across different categories of books—for example, because some are designed to have a much longer shelf life than others—and quality changes over time could be quite different in different categories. But changes in quality and volume (and hence in print runs) are not the only considerations which may affect publishers' costs and prices over time. For example, there is bound to be some improvement in printing technology, or indeed a switch to an innovative process such as 'desktop publishing'.

It is important to bear these provisoes in mind since they render direct comparisons between different price indices a matter for caution. There are currently two main indices in use, although a third, discussed briefly below, whilst it is no longer operative, is worth a mention since it has been used in prior analysis of the book industry.

The Publishers' Association's
Statistics Collection Scheme (PASCS)

PASCS provides information about the number of titles sold, broken down into a variety of categories, and the average price received by the publisher in each category. As indicated above, this needs to be adjusted to take account of changes in retail margins. These have tended to rise during the past decade as bookselling chains have increased their share of the market, which means that prices received by publishers must be adjusted upwards by an increasingly large margin over time.

An additional problem arises insofar as the sample used for calculating prices represents roughly one-half of the industry. Whilst this is statistically significant, the sample is nevertheless much more representative of large publishers than of small, and hence of the categories of book they specialise in.

Stripping out non-net books and concentrating on domestic sales (although calculations taking exports into account produce much the same results), the PASCS figures show considerable variability according to category of book. Whilst the prices of university/professional books tended to move steadily upwards in line with the average during the 1980s, Mass-Market Paperbacks (MMPB) rose irregularly and overall much more

[60]

sharply. By way of contrast, the General category remained constant in money terms, implying a significant reduction after adjusting for inflation. Overall, the average rose significantly faster than the RPI, although the difference was less than that recorded by the other indices discussed below.

The Bookseller Index

This is calculated as a simple average by dividing the total price of all books recorded in the *Bookseller* during a given year by the number of books recorded. The index has a tendency to move in spurts, each followed by a plateau, but the overall trend during the 1980s was a much faster rise than that recorded by the RPI. Since no information on volume is taken into account, the index must be treated with care. In particular, a short print-run book with associated high cost and price is equally weighted compared to a large volume book with associated lower cost and price. Hence, the rapid rise in the average price reflected, in part, the general reduction in print runs during the 1980s and also the sharp rise in advances paid out for potential best-sellers.

The Book Prices Index

This was, until 1986 when it ceased to be calculated separately, the official government index for book prices. It was based upon a sample of book prices collected as part of the data collection process for the RPI. Over the period 1981-86 it rose much faster than the other indices, and outstripped the RPI by such a large margin as to call its validity into question. Its obvious disadvantages were the absence of any adjustment for volume, together with doubts about whether the sample was truly representative, whilst its main virtues were that it was based upon prices paid in bookshops and that it was calculated on a comparable basis to the RPI.

Conclusions

Given the stated drawbacks to the methods used in calculating the above indices, it might be reasonable to conclude that no categoric conclusions are possible. It is necessary to go somewhat beyond that, however, since Fishwick's defence of the NBA (Fishwick, 1989, pp. 34-5 and Appendix 2) reconstructs the PASCS data in such a way as to suggest that the real increase in the prices of net books between 1981 and 1987 was under 4 per cent after adjustment for inflation, and that of consumer books (that is, with university/professional books excluded) was effectively zero.

[61]

The approach used by Fishwick was to select a particular 'basket' of books at one point in time and to calculate how much its price rose during the period under review. It must be recognised, however, that the choice of a particular 'basket' is essentially arbitrary, and that the base year for determining the sequence of prices is also a matter of choice. In this particular case the key issue is the switch away from MMPBs, the prices of which were rising very rapidly during the 1980s, to other categories of books, the prices of which were either rising relatively slowly or even falling. By opting for an early base year, say 1981, the 'basket' contains a high proportion of MMPBs, and hence overstates price rises in relation to the actual 'basket' (containing fewer MMPBs) bought in later years. Fishwick's own calculations used 1985 as the base year, allegedly to correspond to the practice of the Central Statistical Office (CSO). However, it is evident (although Fishwick failed to point it out) that the 'basket' in this much later year in the series contains relatively fewer MMPBs and hence *understates* the price rise since 1981.

It may be argued that more sophisticated statistical techniques are necessary, and that a book price index ought to be calculated on the same basis as the RPI—that is, the PASCS data should be readjusted as a chained Laspeyres index. A calculation along these lines has been done by Dr Ian Preston of Nuffield College, Oxford, for the period 1981-86, and this shows that book prices rose by roughly 20 per cent in real terms. This figure, as previously indicated, is necessarily an understatement because the raw PASCS data is not adjusted for the increase in retail margins during this period. Under the circumstances, *it is not possible to accept the claim that the NBA has been instrumental in holding down book prices. All the evidence is in practice to the contrary, even if there are differences of degree.*

It is also of interest to conjecture whether this will prove to be a continuing trend if the NBA remains in force. A particular point to note in this respect is that the really sharp price rises have been associated with the MMPB category. In recent years the advances offered to the popular authors in this category have continued to escalate, and cross-price elasticity is relatively low because of the drawing power of specific authors. Hence, whilst MMPB sales are a declining proportion of total book sales, the inflationary bias associated with this category is likely to result in book prices outstripping inflation for the foreseeable future.

VIII. THE BOOK TRADE OVERSEAS

The US Experience

In studies of the NBA remarkably little attention is paid to the US market where there has never been any RPM on books. In certain cases, this appears to reflect the (untested) assumption that discounting is so widespread that it has driven independent bookshops out of business. Dr Fishwick, rather curiously, starts by citing evidence that only 22 per cent of books were sold at below list price, a percentage he considers to be surprisingly low (Fishwick, 1989, p. 27), and then goes on to claim that in certain 'medium-sized towns in the USA . . . no current titles were found [by himself] on offer at other than full prices'.

It is the experience of one of the authors, who has travelled extensively in the USA, that discounted books are readily available in what Dr Fishwick may regard as large towns, but for our purposes it is necessary to discuss developments across the USA even though there may be places where their consequences are less evident. What we ultimately seek to discover is whether the US experience is likely to be followed in the UK in the absence of the NBA.

Much of what has gone wrong in the publishing industry in the USA can be laid at the door of the absurd advances being offered to best-selling authors—absurd in the sense that they are frequently not recovered even where the book(s) reach the top of the best-seller list. This phenomenon is by no means confined to the USA. It results from the fact that, whilst it is irrational for a publisher who suspects strongly that he will make a loss by so doing, to pay whatever is demanded by a best-selling author's agent to keep that author with his imprint, or to bribe that author to switch to his imprint, the agent is often able to persuade the publisher that this is a more sensible strategy than having no best-selling authors at all.

Movement Away from Central City Shopping

The roots of the problem lie in the shift away from the centre of American cities during the great era of the motor car after the Second World War. Starved of all their customers, the central bookshops which were accustomed to catering to a very diverse set of tastes were forced to close down. Their place was taken by nationwide chains such as Waldenbooks and B. Dalton, which operated shops in suburban shopping malls. Their potential customers were primarily people who had entered the malls to buy something other than a book. Furthermore, competition for shop space forced the chains to opt for the 'pile-them-high, sell-them-quick' techniques of other consumer product chains. Hence they concentrated upon best-sellers, offered a bibliographic service of such limitations that it could be provided by a cheap, unskilled labour force, and centralised their distribution systems to reduce their overheads.

Sales of best-sellers, predominantly in hardback format, predictably soared, whilst those of more specialised titles with limited mass-market appeal predictably fell away. As time passed, sales of discounted hardbacks came to mirror those of paperback reprints of best-sellers, which were normally distributed on a monthly cycle by magazine wholesalers to newsstands and supermarkets. This monthly cycle necessitated the removal of the previous month's unsold stock.

The sale-or-return principle is well established in the UK as well as in the USA, as noted previously. Because it induces booksellers to hold more stock than they truly expect to sell, it inevitably goes hand-in-hand with heavy returns. In the USA, the book chains could not afford to be out of stock of potential best-sellers, and hence they overstocked on a major sale. If the title took off, the stock would all be sold, but if it failed perhaps one-half of the copies might be returned. Over the years, the percentage of hardback returns in the USA roughly doubled from 12 to 25 per cent. While some of these could be remaindered, which in turn created the need for retail outlets specialising in remaindering hardcover titles, this produced very little revenue for publishers who also had to write off those copies which even the remainder shops could not handle. This had a depressive effect upon the profitability of publishers. Furthermore, the piles of cheap remainders made it difficult to push up the prices of new hardbacks by way of compensation, since that would simply have driven customers who were prepared to wait in order to save money into the remainder bookshops.

Best-Selling Titles

In the case of best-sellers, the key cost is the author's advance, which can run to millions of dollars. Given that a large part of a publisher's list either loses money or, at best, breaks even, profitability and, more importantly, cash flow depend upon the small number of best-sellers which actually cover their authors' advances. Hence, as indicated above, publishers become fixated by the necessity to retain, or to acquire, authors with guaranteed selling power.

Not surprisingly, these authors obeyed the principles of the free market and raised the price for their signature on a contract—in many cases beyond the point at which the advances offered could reasonably be expected to be recoverable. Nevertheless, publishers put up the money. What they failed to appreciate was that, instead of the publisher's imprint playing an instrumental rôle in the volume of sales, as it had traditionally done, their sales were increasingly driven solely by the author's name. In other words, the publisher had increasingly little to do with the traditional editorial aspects of publishing and became increasingly a promoter and distributor.

The big difference between publishing and other businesses was that publishers continued to finance the system through their advances. At the same time, they had to bear the risks inherent in publishing books by unknown authors—yet if any of these became best-sellers the whole cycle would begin again. It is evident that this must act as a destabilising force within the industry. The fact that it took so long to surface can be ascribed to the rapid expansion of the chains, which boosted turnover and hence gave the illusion that spiralling advances would, in most cases, prove a wise investment. However, such an expansion must ultimately slow down, or cease altogether, because new shop sites offering the potential for sufficient turnover become increasingly hard to find.

By the end of the 1980s the period of chain expansion was over. Whilst this period was associated with a number of negative influences on the book market—in particular the narrowing of choice in the chain bookshop and the spiralling of advances, there was also a plus side. This arose because a large number of ordinary individuals, who had previously shunned bookshops, had become used to treating them as just another convenience store. Yet the chain bookstore lacked something which other convenience stores did not, namely, a sufficiently wide array of products to satisfy consumer demand.

The free market, recognising that there was a demand for a different type of bookshop, promptly responded by providing it.

[65]

These bookshops offered a wide inventory of 'serious' literature, including a wide array of backlist books (in print for over one year) as well as current offerings. In this, they were assisted by the collapse of the real estate market in much of America, which helped to make sites available and to reduce overheads.

Rochester, NY: Case Study of the Trend

This trend may be illustrated by the experience of Rochester in New York State. In November 1990, Borders, an Ann-Arbor, Michigan-based bookseller at the forefront of the new trend, opened the company's 12th store in Rochester. Located in a prominent shopping mall in the suburbs, the 14,500 square feet store has a stock of 80,000 titles, five information desks and 23 employees who are tested on their literary knowledge before they are given a job.

The chains themselves have decided to follow this trend. In August 1990, Barnes and Noble, the current owner of B. Dalton, opened the first of a series of superstores (out of a projected total of as many as 20 such outlets) stocking about 100,000 titles, 80,000 more than in an average chain store. Most will open in 1991. Meanwhile, Waldenbooks is embarking upon a major investment programme to convert its 23 Waldenbooks and More stores, which carry videos and other products in addition to books, into large stores called Waldenbooks and More Books with a stock of around 50,000 titles. Crown Books, the third-largest chain, is opening five super-bookstores, and even Tower Records is about to open its first big bookstore.

According to the American Booksellers' Association, sales in US bookstores grew by 63 per cent between 1982 and 1987, as against a rise of 44 per cent for all retail sales. Furthermore, the *number* of bookshops grew by 12 per cent, twice the rate for all retail establishments. Of the 10,000 bookshops (not including variety and magazine stores), some 7,000 are independently owned. On the whole, therefore, the current position is a healthy one, even though it has taken a period of structural adjustment to arrive at it.

Experience in France

The experience of RPM on books in France is indicative of why the 1962 Judgement greatly over-estimated the detriment to be expected in the event of the abolition of the NBA. Traditionally, publishers supplied books with a recommended retail price within margins set by the government. However, in the mid-1970s, the discount chain FNAC began selling books at prices below the recommended levels, a policy subsequently taken up by some department stores. In July 1979 publishers were obliged to abandon recommended prices, thereby permitting bookshops to sell at any price they chose.

Subsequently, many booksellers found price to be inelastic, and only department stores with an emphasis upon best-sellers profited from this new-found freedom. As a result, most stock-holding booksellers voted for a return to recommended prices. RPM was reintroduced under the Lang Act of 1981. It remains in force and was confirmed by the publication of the Arts Ministry's Cahart Report in 1988 which favoured RPM. Despite this, when in April 1989 the Finance Ministry published a study of the economic effects of the Lang Act, it concluded that the Act was against the interests of consumers.

The immediate effect of the Lang Act was to cause the retail prices of books to rise, which is understandable given that FNAC had previously been offering discounts of up to 20 per cent off retail prices. In the early 1980s book prices easily outran the consumer price index, although they subsequently moved into approximate equivalence. It is argued that this relatively sharp rise in book prices was not a direct consequence of the Lang Act, but rather reflected the need to readjust after a period of disequilibrium. Nevertheless, the price effect was contrary to that expressed in the Judgement.

During the years prior to the Lang Act, concentration in French bookselling was on the decline, whereas it rose to its previous level in the years subsequent to the passing of the Act. What appears to have happened is that the outlawing of recommended prices prior to 1981 permitted outlets to be opened up, away from major population centres, which could charge relatively high, and hence reasonably profitable, price levels. The reimposition of RPM was, therefore, damaging to the prospects of these outlets, again in contradiction to the predictions of the Judgement.

The French experience suggests that the abolition of the NBA will lead to more, rather than fewer, book outlets. Publishers in the UK, in the absence of the NBA, may still seek to maintain recommended prices, in which case the French experience may not be replicated. Nevertheless, neither the

[67]

French experience, nor that of Australia where initial closures were quickly compensated by the opening of new outlets, gives reason to expect the severe consequences predicted in the Judgement.

IX. CONCLUSION

The NBA has been a fact of life in the publishing industry for a good many decades. The industry, or more specifically its Associations, have fought a long rearguard action to keep it in existence, so far with success. Our purpose in writing this *Paper* is not to suggest that the case put forward to support the NBA is wholly without merit, nor indeed to suggest that the historic structure of the industry and its practices present an easy target to be shot down by those who are sceptical about the NBA's merits.

Rather, we have set out to demonstrate that the arguments used to justify the NBA have lost their force as the industry has evolved in the context of an economy where resale price maintenance is otherwise absent. The recurrent cry of 'books are different' sounds increasingly hollow when, despite superficial adherence to the NBA, industry practices, for example the development of specialised book clubs, or sale or return clauses, are themselves destroying some of the foundations upon which the case in favour of the NBA was built.

We have examined the underlying economic arguments used by defendants of the NBA and found them wanting. We have examined the database on such matters as changes in prices over time and concluded that there are strong grounds for a re-interpretation less favourable to the retention of the NBA. We have examined overseas experience and concluded that, whilst there will inevitably be some short-term dislocation if the NBA is abolished, it will not have the dire long-term consequences predicted by its supporters.

There is simply no good reason to treat the NBA as the exception that proves the rule. Many in the book trade have admitted as much in private for many years past. In recent months there have been increasing public signs that the NBA will soon have run its course. The actions by Dillons were unlikely to prove terminal in isolation. So long as W. H. Smith, with its substantial market power, gave the NBA its whole-hearted support, no other market participant could be expected to carry the day.

[69]

It now appears, however, that W. H. Smith has been negotiating with major imprints such as Random Century and HarperCollins to permit bookshops to cut the price of best-sellers by as much as 25 per cent. Like most other industries, publishing is suffering badly during the current recession and, given fixed prices, volume reductions go hand-in-hand with equal reductions in revenue.

The time is clearly ripe to test the hypothesis that the industry will prosper in the context of flexible prices. The demise of the NBA could be temporary since there is nothing to prevent its restoration, either as a matter of law or of commercial practice (although it is rumoured that its demise may be proposed in the forthcoming Conservative manifesto). Nevertheless, in reality, it is either adhered to by all major market participants or it is not. If the industry is truly divided, the NBA cannot survive. Cartels, whether explicit or implicit, are difficult to put back together again. It is, therefore, reasonable to suppose that any temporary demise of the NBA will also prove to be terminal.

SUMMARY

1. The Net Book Agreement dates back to 1957, and was examined in the Restrictive Practices Court in 1962. The Judgement was favourable on the grounds that abolition would (a) reduce the number of stockholding bookshops and the size of their stocks, (b) cause book prices to rise, and (c) cause the number of titles published to fall.

2. The NBA was not considered to be an instrument for fixing minimum prices. Its abolition was expected to transfer demand from one outlet to another rather than to increase the size of the aggregate market for books. The NBA was held to be compatible with innovatory methods of selling books.

3. None of these arguments has withstood the test of time. The introduction of 'sale or return' conditions by publishers has, in particular, much reduced the risk of over-stocking by bookshops, thus enabling them, in the absence of the NBA, to introduce the practice, normal in other retail trades, of opting for a low price-high volume selling strategy.

4. In the absence of price competition bookshops substitute non-price competition irrespective of the customers' wishes. The (politicians') desire to restore market power to customers has led to the abolition of resale price maintenance in all retail sectors with the effective exception of bookselling. Innovation in bookselling is stifled because cost savings cannot be passed on to customers.

5. Publishers therefore operate what amounts to a cartel since book prices are geared to the 'going rate' for a mass-market paperback or academic text. Arguments about the contestability of the market for books greatly exaggerate the potential for entry once distribution problems are taken into account.

6. The elasticity conditions operating in the market for books are nothing like as adverse as is claimed by proponents of the NBA, and do not differ greatly from other retail markets. In addition, title output has exploded over the past decade. It is hard to understand why fewer books would cause a consumer detriment. There is no reason to believe that the 'higher reaches of literature' would suffer disproportionately from any cutback.

7. The growth of book clubs has effectively introduced heavy discounting into the book market, even for new publications. Equally, 'own brand' sales are a form of implicit discounting. Denying the same discounting opportunity to retailers is perverse.

8. Modern chain bookstores hold much larger stocks than they did a decade ago. They are much better able to withstand the consequences of price competition and could easily boost turnover largely by attracting more customers, by means of discounting, who then make multiple purchases.

9. Rigorous examination of data on book prices indicates that they have outstripped the Retail Prices Index over the past decade. This is especially true of mass-market paperbacks. The NBA therefore appears to have failed to hold down prices despite claims to the contrary.

10. Overseas experience where price maintenance has been abolished lends no support to the proposition that it is a necessary condition for the existence of a healthy book market. This is especially true of the USA.

APPENDIX:
THE NET BOOK AGREEMENT 1957

We, the undersigned several firms of publishers, being desirous in so far as we publish books at net prices (as to which each publisher is free to make his own decisions), those net prices shall normally be the prices at which such books are sold to the public as hereinafter defined, and in order to avoid dis-organisation in the book trade and to ensure that the public may be informed of and able uniformly to take advantage of the conditions under which net books may be sold at less than the net prices, hereby agree to adopt and each of us does hereby adopt the following standard sale conditions for the net books published by us within the United Kingdom.

Standard Conditions of Sale of Net Books

(i)   Except as provided in clauses (ii) and (iv) hereof and except as we may otherwise direct, net books shall not be sold or offered for sale or caused or permitted to be sold or offered for sale to the public at less than the net published prices.

(ii) A net book may be sold or offered for sale to the public at less than the net published price if

    (a) it has been held in stock by the bookseller for a period of more than twelve months from the date of the latest purchase by him of any copy thereof and

    (b) it has been offered to the publisher at cost price or at the proposed reduced price whichever shall be the lower and such offer has been refused by the publisher.

(iii) A net book may be sold or offered for sale to the public at less than the net published price if it is second-hand and six months have elapsed since its date of publication.

(iv) A net book may be sold at a discount to such libraries, book agents (including Service Unit libraries), quantity buyers and institutions as are from time to time authorised by the Council of The Publishers' Association of such amount and on such conditions as are laid down in the instrument of authorisation. Such amount and conditions shall not initially be less favourable than those prevailing at the time of this Agreement.

(v) For the purposes of clause (i) hereof a book shall be considered as sold at less than the net published price if the bookseller

(a) offers or gives any consideration in cash to any purchaser except under license from the Council of The Publishers' Association or

(b) offers or gives any consideration in kind (e.g. card indexing, stamping, reinforced bindings, etc.) at less than the actual cost thereof to the bookseller.

(vi) For the purposes of this Agreement and of these Standard Conditions: *Net book* shall mean a book, pamphlet, map or other similar printed matter published at a net price. *Net price* and *net published price* shall mean the price fixed from time to time by the publisher below which the net book shall not be sold to the public.

Public shall be deemed to include schools, libraries, institutions and other non-trading bodies.

Person shall include any company, firm, corporation, club, institution, organisation, association or other body.

(vii) The above conditions shall apply to all sales executed in the United Kingdom and the Republic of Ireland whether effected by wholesaler or retailer when the publisher's immediate trade customer, whether wholesaler or retailer, or the wholesaler's immediate trade customer, is in the United Kingdom or the Republic of Ireland.

We, the undersigned several firms of publishers further agree to appoint and each of does hereby appoint the Council of The Publishers' Association to act as our agent in the collection of information concerning breaches of contract by persons selling or offering for sale net books, and in keeping each individual publisher informed of breaches in respect of such net books as are published by him, and we further hereby undertake and agree that we will each enforce our contractual rights and our rights under the Restrictive Trade Practices Act 1956 if called

[74]

upon to do so by the Council of The Publishers' Association, and provided that we shall be indemnified by The Publishers' Association if so requested by us in respect of any costs incurred by us or by the Council of The Publishers' Association on our behalf.

SELECT BIBLIOGRAPHY

Barker, R. E., and G. R. Davies (eds.) (1966), *Books Are Different*, London: Macmillan.

Book Industry Study Group (BISG) (annual), *Book Trends*, Scranton: BISG.

Cahart, C. F. (1987), *Le Livre Français, a-t-il un Avenir?*, Paris: Documentation Française.

Calvani, T., and J. Largenfeld (1985), 'An overview of the current debate on resale price maintenance', *Contemporary Policy Issues*, Spring.

CEC (1982), 'Decision relating to Case IV/428', VBBB/VBVB, OJEC, L54/36, 25 February.

CEC (1989), 'Decision relating to cases IV/27.393 and IV/27.394, Publishers' Association—Net Book Agreement', OJEC, L22/12, 21 January.

Cohen, R. (1990), 'If the written word is really dying, who is patronizing the "superstores"?', *The New York Times*, 30 September.

Comanor, W. S., and J. B. Kirkwood (1985), 'Resale price maintenance and anti-trust policy', *Contemporary Policy Issues*, Spring.

Consumers' Association (1978), *The Net Book Agreement*. A *Which?* Campaign Report, Consumers' Association, 24 March.

Curwen, P. J. (1977), 'The economics of academic publishing in the UK', *The Journal of Industrial Economics*, March.

Curwen, P. J. (1981), *The UK Publishing Industry*, Oxford: Pergamon.

Dept. of Trade and Industry (1988), *Review of Restrictive Trade Practices Policy—a Consultative Document*, Cm. 331, London: HMSO.

Dillons (1989), *Submission to the Office of Fair Trading on the Net Book Agreement*,

Ecalle, F. (1988), 'Une évaluation de la loi du 10 août 1981 relative au prix du livre', Paris: *Économie et Prévision*, 5/88.

Ellis, R. (1988), 'Hidden block on cheap books', *The Sunday Times*, 10 April.

Euromonitor (annual), *The Book Report*, London: Euromonitor Publications.

Fishwick, F., and D. Preston (1982), *Book Publishing and Distribution*, Brussels: Commission of the European Communities.

Fishwick, F. (1985), *Book Prices in Australia and North America*, Brussels: Commission of the European Communities.

Fishwick, F. (1989), *The Economic Implications of the Net Book Agreement*, London: Publishers' Association.

Gould, J. R., and L. E. Preston (1965), 'Resale price maintenance and retail outlets', *Economica*, August.

Hay, D., and J. Vickers (1988), 'The reform of UK competition policy', *National Institute Economic Review*, August.

Hill, L. (1978), 'An insight into the finances of the record industry', *Three Banks Review*, Vol. 118, pp. 28-45.

Hughes, N. (1977), 'Does the trade still want the Net Book Agreement?', *The Bookseller*, No. 3,736, pp. 462-66.

Jenkins, S. (1988), 'Personal view', *The Sunday Times*, 17 April.

MacArthur, B. (1990), 'Shocker has book trade quaking in its covers', *The Sunday Times*, 14 October.

Maher, T. (1989), 'Net Book Agreement—the case for abrogation', *The Bookseller*, 17 February.

Marvel, H. P., and S. McCafferty (1986), 'The political economy of resale price maintenance', *Journal of Political Economy*, October.

Morris, D. (1977), 'The economics of the Net Book Agreement. A re-evaluation', Discussion Paper No. 53, University of Nottingham, Dept. of Industrial Economics.

Nieuwenhuysen, J. P. (1975), *Competition in Australian Bookselling*, Melbourne: Melbourne University Press.

[77]

Norrie, I. (1979), 'My own and other sacred cows', *The Bookseller*, No. 3,673, pp. 2,312-14.

Pickering, J. (1969), 'Would prices rise without rpm?', *Oxford Economic Papers*, Vol. 21(2).

Publishers' Association (BMC) (1980), *Impulse Buying of Books*, London: Publishers' Association.

Skeoch, L. A. (1964), 'The abolition of resale price maintenance: some notes on the Canadian Experience', *Economica*, pp. 260-69.

Urry, M. (1988), 'The march of the multiples', *Financial Times*, 9 March.

Vickers, J., and D. Hay (1987), *The Economics of Market Dominance*, Oxford: Blackwell.

Williams, J. (1988), 'Book prices coming unbound', *The Sunday Times*, 2 October.

Yamey, B. S. (1960), *Resale Price Maintenance and Shoppers' Choice*, Hobart Paper No. 1, London: Institute of Economic Affairs, 3rd Edition 1964.

Yamey, B. S. (ed.) (1966), *Resale Price Maintenance*, London: Weidenfeld and Nicolson.

Zifcak, M. (1977), 'Net Book Agreement. An Australian view', *The Bookseller*, No. 3,744, pp. 2,156-57.

Zifcak, M. (1978), 'Do booksellers need resale price maintenance?', *The Bookseller*, No. 3,787, pp. 3,332-35.

RECENTLY PUBLISHED BY THE IEA
Beyond Universities:
A New Republic of the Intellect
SIR DOUGLAS HAGUE, CBE

Summary

Universities in the UK have traditionally operated under a common system which institutionalises important restrictive practices. They have operated in a cartel whose output has been regulated by government. The individual firms (i.e. universities) are allocated quotas of students by government, and fees and salaries are set in ways that are typical of a classic cartel. The university cartel is underpinned by a further monopoly, granted as of right to each university. In the UK nobody can award degrees unless empowered to do so by royal charter or by the Secretary of State for Education and Science.

Professor Sir Douglas Hague takes this argument a stage further by stating that the current stage of economic development is strongly based on the acquisition, analysis and transmission of information and on its application. Universities will therefore be forced to share, or even give up, part of their role as repositories of information and as power bases for ideas transmitted through teaching and writing.

In this richly original *Hobart Paper*, Professor Sir Douglas Hague identifies the challenges which universities will have to meet and argues that, if these can be overcome, universities should be able to survive both as competitors and complements of the knowledge industries over the coming decades.

The Author

Professor Sir Douglas Hague, CBE, is Honorary Visiting Professor at Manchester Business School, where he was previously Professor of Managerial Economics and Deputy Director. He is author of numerous works on economics and management, and was Chairman of the Economic and Social Research Council, 1983-87. (A full note on the author can be found on page 8.)

ISBN 0-255 36244-7   Hobart Paper 115

IEA   **The Institute of Economic Affairs**
2 Lord North Street, Westminster
London SW1P 3LB

£6.95   Telephone: 071-799 3745

The Wealth of Nations and the Environment

MIKHAIL S. BERNSTAM

Several years ago it would have been difficult to gain acceptance for the view that capitalism was more environmentally friendly than other economic systems. It would follow that a non-capitalist economy offers better safeguards for the environment.

The fall of the Iron Curtain has unveiled environmental devastation far exceeding the alleged excesses of present-day market economies. The dismal economic performance of socialist and communist economies has been achieved at high costs to the environment and the health of their citizens.

In this fascinating *Occasional Paper*, rich in examples, evidence and analysis, Mikhail Bernstam shows that the pursuit of profit in a capitalist economy leads to a husbanding of resources. Mature capitalist economies use fewer resources to produce the equivalent level of output and hence do less damage to the environment. The findings of this paper will surprise many, anger some, but challenge all of us.

ISBN 0-255 36240-4

Occasional Paper 85

£6.95

The Institute of Economic Affairs
2 Lord North Street, Westminster
London SW1P 3LB
Telephone: 071-799 3745

IEA PUBLICATIONS
Subscription Service

An annual subscription is the most convenient way to obtain our publications. Every title we produce in all our regular series will be sent to you immediately on publication and without further charge, representing a substantial saving.

Individual subscription rates*

Britain: £30·00 p.a. including postage.
£28·00 p.a. if paid by Banker's Order.
£18·00 p.a. to teachers and students who pay *personally.*

Europe: £30·00 p.a. including postage.

South America: £40·00 p.a. or equivalent.

Other Countries: Rates on application. In most countries subscriptions are handled by local agents. Addresses are available from the IEA.

* These rates are *not* available to companies or to institutions.

To: The Treasurer, Institute of Economic Affairs,
2 Lord North Street, Westminster,
London SW1P 3LB

I should like to subscribe from ....

I enclose a cheque/postal order for:

☐ £30·00

☐ £18·00   I am a teacher/student at ....

....

☐ Please send a Banker's Order form.

☐ Please send an invoice.

☐ Please charge my credit card:

Please tick   ☐ **VISA**   ☐ 🅰   ☐ **AMERICAN EXPRESS**   ☐ Ⓓ

Card No: ☐☐☐☐☐☐☐☐☐☐☐☐☐☐☐☐☐☐

In addition I would like to purchase the following previously published titles:

....

....

Name ....

Address ....   ⎫
                                                                              ⎬ BLOCK
....   ⎪ LETTERS
                                                                              ⎪ PLEASE
.... Post Code ....   ⎭

Signed .... Date ....

HP116